WHEN
RELIGION GETS SICK

WHEN
RELIGION GETS SICK

by
Wayne E. Oates

THE WESTMINSTER PRESS
Philadelphia

1970.

ISBN 0–664–24891–8

LIBRARY OF CONGRESS CATALOG CARD NO. 76–114727

BOOK DESIGN BY
DOROTHY ALDEN SMITH

Published by The Westminster Press ®
Philadelphia, Pennsylvania

PRINTED IN THE UNITED STATES OF AMERICA

To
WILLIAM KELLER, M.D.
EDWARD E. LANDIS, M.D.
ROGER K. WHITE, M.D.
REBECCA GASS, R.N.

CONTENTS

ACKNOWLEDGMENTS

I SHOULD LIKE TO EXPRESS MY APPRECIATION to the Trustees of the Southern Baptist Theological Seminary, who saw to it that I had a sabbatical leave in which to work with the faculty of the Department of Psychiatry of the University of Louisville Medical School in the development of the ideas set forth in this book. A debt of gratitude is due to the staff of the Norton Memorial Infirmary Psychiatric Clinic, a teaching unit of the Department of Psychiatry of the Medical School, for collaborating with me in the development of these thoughts. Special thanks are due William Keller, M.D.; Edward E. Landis, M.D., Medical Director; Roger K. White, M.D., Clinical Director; and Miss Rebecca Gass, R.N., Nursing Supervisor. Likewise, Mrs. George Stritikus, my teaching assistant, was of continuing assistance to me in the work associated with the creation of this book.

Furthermore, my graduate seminar worked with me during the better part of the fall of 1969 in a patient review of each of the chapters, making valuable suggestions for the revision of the first draft of the book. The students are as follows: Ernest Cowger, Frank Dawkins,

Franklin Duncan, Martha Gray, Herman Green, Jack Grisham, T. W. Johnson, Colin Kruesch, Donald McGuire, Edwin Nash, James Pollard, and Paul Turner. These persons are not only fine students, but they have been junior colleagues in the search for the nature of sick religion and wholeness of the life that man lives before God.

W.E.O.

Norton Psychiatric Clinic
Louisville, Kentucky

WHEN
RELIGION GETS SICK

Chapter 1

WHEN RELIGION
GETS SICK

A GUILT-LADEN MAN gouges his eyes out because he has read literally the Biblical injunction, "If thine eye offend thee, pluck it out . . ."

I am walking down the corridor of a mental health center with the superintendent of the institution. We see a young girl with her right hand missing. He tells me that she felt that God had told her to cut her offending hand off and she did so.

My students saw an eleven-year-old boy in a juvenile detention center. He had been placed there by his parents. He is the oldest child of four living at home. He would not stay at home but insisted on running away. He would stay out of school and go to work with a nearby neighbor, who was a contractor building houses. He would work all day installing dry wall under the direction of the man. If the boy ran away from home in the evening, he would be found late at night helping an auto mechanic repair cars. The parents' complaint against him was that he was unmanageable and would not go to the new school where they were sending him. They wanted the public authorities to "make him mind."

When my students investigated the home situation, they found that the school to which the boy had previously gone was a Catholic school and that now he had to go to a public school. When the students inquired as to why the schools had been changed, they discovered it was because the parents had become "gifted with the Holy Spirit," had changed churches from the Catholic Church to a pentecostal-type church, and were demanding that the boy "get right with God" and have an "experience with the Holy Spirit." They had told him, the father said, that he would never be right with them until he got right with God. The father was angry with the son because he refused to "knuckle under" to God. A sixteen-year-old son had left the home, had a part-time job, and continued his attendance at the Catholic school.

These instances convince us that the term "religious" is very ambiguous, and that, like the word "love," it covers a multitude of sins. Since the apostle Paul stood on Mars' Hill and told the Athenians that they were in all things very religious, the term "religion" has had a double meaning. It can refer to a very positive, "health-giving" doctrine by which men not only survive but live and do well. A healthy faith is the expression of the total personality of an individual in his relationship to the Divine as his ultimate and comprehensive loyalty. At the same time, "religion" can refer to a pantheon of false gods by which men shrivel in the bondage of fear and death. When religion becomes reified—that is, made a thing of as separate and apart from the total expression of the whole life of a person—it becomes an external "it," a thing apart. When this happens, the "it" religion becomes either a segregated, autonomous system in an airtight compartment separated from the rest of life, or it becomes a disturbing factor in the total functioning of the person. // In either instance, it is sick. In these latter instances, a person's "religion" becomes "bad news" instead of good news. Such religion is sick and not well. When we use the word "religion," then, we are not *necessarily* saying that something is good.

Persons come to pastors when their religion has become a burden to them. When they are sick at heart because they are becoming more and more religious but enjoying God less and less, people have a way of turning to their pastor. Their pastor may be in something of the same "fix" himself; nevertheless, he is called upon by people when their religion gets sick. The concern I have in writing this book is to enable both the pastor and the persons who come to him to understand the religiously sick. This book is only secondarily about mental illness. It is primarily about sick religion.

THE INTENTIONS OF THIS BOOK

Basic questions provide the intentions of this book: When does religion get sick? What kinds of experiences blight the religious lives of individuals, groups, and their leaders? What can the pastor and his church do about these experiences when they occur? How can they go about predicting when sick religion will occur and preventing this malaise of the spiritual life from setting in? These questions imply that religion may be either sick or well and that it is not always one or the other. Ordinarily, it is sick in some respects and well in others at the same time. This view keeps us from the intellectual "dead ends" of Freud's assumption that religion is a universal neurosis at all times and places. It also avoids the sweet optimism of denominationalism in American religion; that is, that religion, because it *is* religious, *has* to be well, good, and healthy by the nature of the case. Both kinds of thinking are unrealistic and do not fit the facts of life.

SOURCES OF INFORMATION

This book is based on several sources of information. The first is fifty cases continuous over a period of a year or more of patients and their families treated *by a minister* in consultation with a psychiatrist, psychiatric residents, a clinical psychologist, two social workers, and a social-group worker in a psychiatric clinic. Care will be taken to protect the privacy of patients. Case history and not piecemeal reference will be the methodology used.

A second source of information is empirical studies of mentally ill persons whose lives are predominantly characterized by their religious concern. These clinical studies will be drawn from published reports by physicians, psychologists, and clinically trained ministers, who have recorded their data in reputable journals of a scholarly nature. These studies will be reported in detail but with as little technicality as possible. The journal material on the subject will fall into several categories, of which only two kinds will be used here.

Four types of literature can be noted that will, nevertheless, not be used because of the nature of the method of study being observed. These types of articles are: (1) articles of a general, nonspecific philosophical nature about the relation of religion and medicine; (2) articles referring to either a philosophy or a theology of medicine; (3) articles that deal with the general problems of relating religion and psychiatry, such as cross-cultural studies of religion that have been done by physicians.

Two kinds of literature will be used:

1. The first kind of article is the empirical study of a number of cases with a statistical profile approach to the religious concerns of the patients. The June, 1969, issue of the *American Journal of Psychiatry* has such a study of the relative effects of the religious backgrounds on the mourning process in the lives of widows in Japan.

2. The most valuable kind of research article for this study is a case history study of one or more patients whose emotional disorders were interwoven with the religious concerns of the patient. A. W. Kushner writes such an article under the title "Two Cases of Autocastration Due to Religious Delusions," in the *British Journal of Medical Psychology,* Volume 11, July, 1967.

The third source of information upon which this book is based is the autobiographies of persons who have been deeply concerned religiously and who have also suffered deeply from emotional disorders. The autobiographical method has been a classic approach to the problems of religious experience since the time of Augustine's *Confessions.* As one mental patient said in her own autobiographical comment, "Our religion has suffered with the rest of the life of the mental patient."

THE MEANING OF "SICK"

Conclusions are drawn here as to the nature and functioning of "sick" religion. When I use the word "sick," I

am not using it in some broad, vague, generalized sense.
As Prof. H. Stuart Hughes has said, it becomes very much
the "in" thing to do to view society as a whole in terms
of emotional illness and as "sick." Yet he says that this is
so vague as to be meaningless. (*Psychiatric News,* Vol. 4,
No. 6, June, 1969, p. 4.) Rather, when I use the word
"sick" here I am referring to a specific functional break-
down. When religion is sick, it massively hinders the basic
functions of life. Malfunction, then, is the criterion of
sickness. When a person not only fasts according to shared
and spiritually understood "ground rules," but refuses to
eat at all because he fears God's punishment for eating,
then that person has failed to function in a "well" manner. When a person refuses to rest at all because he must
awaken people at every hour of every night of the week
to win them to Christ, the people around him ask if he is
really well. When a person feels that *all* contact of *any*
kind between the sexes is of itself evil when practiced by
anyone, especially himself, then one asks about the illness
or health of the ethical perspective of that person. When
a person's work routine is completely hindered by the
kind of religious life he leads, he has no adequate way of
being a responsible supporter of his family. Then one
asks if he does not have need of the physician as well as
of the Divine.

In other words, the word "sick" is not used in some
global, vague, or moralistic sense here. It does not necessarily refer to "society as the patient" or to the solution
of all the world's problems in some sort of cure-all.
Rather, it refers to specific situations in which particular
people suffer major failures of functioning in the conduct
of their lives because of religious preoccupations and

stumbling blocks. In other words, when the word "sick" is used, it is employed in a restricted rather than a general or "broadside" sense.

A CLINICAL MANUAL OF RELIGIOUS PATHOLOGY

An underlying hope of this writer is to arrive at a distinctly religious understanding of the problems of disturbed and unhappy people. This is not to put the religious understanding over against the psychiatric interpretation of the ills of humankind. Rather, I hope to develop a set of working hypotheses and concepts concerning human behavior in its direst distresses that will be readily understood and appropriated by any minister who has taken the Judeo-Christian interpretation of human life seriously. At the same time, my objective is to cut across the orthodox psychiatric classifications and to produce a religious classification, interpretation, and pattern of approach. Nevertheless, this pattern of approach will not be contrary to nor ignore the demonstrated findings of contemporary psychiatry and psychotherapy. In other words, this is a religious interpretation of the disturbed person's life. As an interpretation, it is just that: *one* interpretation. Whether it becomes a pervasive and influential interpretation depends upon its fidelity to the facts of life it represents and upon how seriously the reader takes these categories of and approaches to understanding and counseling the religiously sick.

The following pages are really statements of working hypotheses concerning a pathology of religion. They are stated in the language and mood of hypothesis. Persons who are looking for statistical and quantitative exactitude will find some comfort, but it will be cold. The realm of interpretation does not always lend itself to precise quantification. Rather, the patterns of interpretation set forth seek to provide working themes that can be tested by students and pastors as they see for themselves whether the hypotheses set forth here fit the kinds of empirical experience they are having. Do they make sense?

THE MINISTER AS A PROFESSIONAL INTERPRETER OF RELIGIOUS PATHOLOGY

The role of the minister is that of an interpreter and evaluator. He is called upon to use his specific skills in understanding and counseling with the distinctly religious concerns of the emotionally disturbed. The value systems of a disturbed person are the minister's "territory." He cannot act as if no one else can have free traffic into and out of this territory; neither, if he is doing his job well, can he assume that anyone else should be the guide rather than he in this territory. He cannot ditch his responsibility on social workers, psychiatrists, and psychologists and whine because they are uninformed and unskilled at dealing with the distinctly religious concerns of persons. He cannot be timid or apologetic about occupying his own territory as a professionally trained person who also "knows his stuff." He can neither be an intimidator of nor be intimidated by persons who are uninformed as to his own training and professional "know-how."

The minister takes the religious problems of persons as real. They are clues to and linkages with the rest of the personal concerns and the social situation of the person who has the ideas. They are not just symptoms of something else. They are valid in and of themselves. As such they are ways of interpreting life so that it makes some sort of sense. If these ways of interpretation are sick, then the whole body will be filled with darkness. The minister and the doctor who take these religious ideas and problems of the person seriously will find in them the patient's way of communicating his distress. For many patients, this is their *only* way to communicate their distress, and to "shut them up" at this point is to consign them to oblivion and ourselves to ineffectiveness. Edgar Draper has said that the patient individualizes his religious communication regardless of what his formal religious background has been. "Details of their interpretations of religion not only fit with their diagnostic picture, but also offered clues to diagnosis at the clinical, developmental, and psychodynamic levels." (Edgar Draper, George Meyer, Zane Parzen, and Gene Samuelson, "On the Diagnostic Value of Religious Ideation," *Archives of General Psychiatry*, Vol. 13, No. 3, Sept., 1965, p. 202.) The patient's religious ideas are symbolic counterparts of this whole life experience and not mere side effects of his "real" condition. They provide the basis for a symptomatic character diagnosis. They are realizable clues for diagnosis of the psychiatric disorder of the patient.

Therefore, the minister and the psychiatrist who will take seriously the religious culture of the patient will have here one more royal road to the hidden agendas of disturbed people's lives. With both the family physician and the attending psychiatrist taking the religious life of the patient as significant in its own right, the total life of the patient is benefited. The physician can no longer afford to consider the religious concern of the

patient as unreal. Nor can the minister ignore that the
religious life of the patient can become ill. Neither religion nor illness is a myth and both may be synonymous.
A realistic approach brings both together in collaboration.

The person who is suffering is comforted and his trust
is established when he knows that his beliefs and cherished
values, however inflamed with illness, are taken seriously
by both his doctor and his minister. He is not ignored as
a religious person by his doctor. He is not treated as
"some sort of nut" by his minister as if his religion did
not matter at all. Standing together, both the minister
and the doctor can more adequately stand by the patient
and take him more seriously.

Chapter 2

IDOLATRY
AND SICK RELIGION

THE MINISTER, by the nature of his calling, is committed to proclaiming the good news of a prophetic faith. In both the Christian and the Jewish heritages, prophetic faith is set over against their own cultural forms, which are by definition idolatrous. In other world religions, a similar obscuring of the ultimate values takes place by excessive preoccupation with the proximate, temporary things that men overvalue. The hypothesis of this chapter is that when the relative values of life take the place of the eternal and ultimate ones, a condition of idolatry exists. The person in this time and place is on the way to becoming off-center, disturbed, unbalanced, and sick at the core of his religious life.

The astute reader will readily ask: "Who is to define what is idolatry and what is the true and living God? Is this not a very relative matter?" "Are you taking a hard, party-line position that gives you the right to determine who the true and living God is and requires that everyone be in accord with this or be seen as sick religiously?" These are very legitimate questions. The answer to them is possible but not easy. The questions can be approached

confessionally as to who *I* think is the true and living God.
The end result would be that as a Christian I *could* be
heard to take a "hard, party line." Or, I can take the
position of a psychologist of religion and ask for an empirical description of the *kind of religious sentiment* that
makes for health and disease in religion. This does not
require that I give specific content and character to the
kind of religion a person may have. It does require a functional value judgment as to *how* the value works. I choose
to follow the latter procedure. The reason for doing so
is that I may speak to people of all religious persuasions
and ask whether they are sick or well in their faith. Even
so, I have already spoken in other places, especially in my
book *Christ and Selfhood,* from an unequivocally Christian point of view. Readers who wish to "positionize" me,
for better or worse, can read that book against the background of what is said here. But, in this book, the distinctly phenomenological and empirical point of view is
taken. What, then, are the characteristics of a religious
world view that could be characterized as laying hold
of the Eternal, and what are the characteristics of an idolatrous religion?

THEOLOGICAL PERSPECTIVES

Paul Tillich has done most to make the concept of the
demonic power of idolatry a negotiable concept for the
modern, sophisticated reader. He says that the distinctly
religious quest is concerned with the power of the New
Being in that which takes the empirical form of an ultimate, not a proximate concern. When we invest ultimate
concern in that which is ultimate, we have anxiety but

it is normal anxiety, which grows out of our realization of our finitude, our mortality in the face of death, and our encounter with meaninglessness in the proximate things of life. When we invest ultimate concern, however, in proximate, finite, temporal, and transitory realities, we "absolutize the finite." We give ourselves over to these proximate concerns, which become idols in our lives. As such, the idol exercises demonic power over us. It has become *the* ultimate power over us. It possesses us with a frail hand. (Illustrations for these ideas rush to my mind, but these can wait for the empirical histories of patients who have become sick in this way.) Nevertheless, the end result is pathological anxiety. (Paul Tillich, *The Courage to Be,* pp. 40–63; Yale University Press, 1952.) The person becomes "pathologically fixed to a limited self-affirmation." (*Ibid.,* p. 73.)

Tillich uses the example of the idolatrous character of utopianism, which serves to make his point very concrete in the face of the almost millennialistic social reform movements of today. He says:

> For utopianism, taken literally, is idolatrous. It gives the quality of ultimacy to something preliminary. It makes unconditional what is conditioned (a future historical situation) and at the same time disregards the always present existential estrangement and the ambiguities of life and history. (Paul Tillich, *Systematic Theology,* Vol. III, p. 355; The University of Chicago Press, 1963.)

Again, Tillich identifies religious nationalism as a contemporary idolatry at the same time that he defines what idolatry is:

Idolatry is the elevation of a preliminary concern to ultimacy. Something essentially conditioned is taken as unconditional, something essentially partial is boosted into universality, and something essentially finite is given infinite significance (the best example is the contemporary idolatry of religious nationalism). (Paul Tillich, *Systematic Theology*, Vol. I, p. 13; The University of Chicago Press, 1951.)

Emil L. Fackenheim, a Jewish professor of philosophy at the University of Toronto, says that a particular symbol or art object is rarely thought of as a modern possibility of idolatry. However, the idolater of today is concerned with living idols that can literally hear, speak, and act. He defines modern idolatry as follows:

The idol itself is divine. The idolatrous projection of infinite feeling upon finite object is such as to produce not a symbolic, but, rather, a literal and hence total identification of finiteness and infinitude. (Emil L. Fackenheim, "Idolatry as a Modern Religious Possibility," in Donald R. Cutler, ed., *The Religious Situation: 1968*, p. 275; Beacon Press, Inc., 1968.)

From a psychological point of view, one can readily discern that the mechanism of idolatrous construction is projection of both wish and fear upon an external person who hears, speaks, and acts. From our understanding of primitive religion, this can be either a living or a dead person, depending upon the sick person's attitude toward death. The ghosts of the restless dead, as in *Hamlet*, can still be operative in the spiritual distemper of the religiously sick. A disturbed and imminently suicidal Saul can consult with the departed spirit of Samuel. Even though he had "cut off the mediums and the wizards from the land" himself, Saul consulted a woman who was a medium and asked her to bring up Samuel for him (I Sam. 28:8 ff.). He did this in disguise, thereby rejecting to a great degree his role as the king. The point, in brief, is that he and Hamlet both were fixed in their loyalty upon a departed and dead hero. Yet, as Fackenheim says, their relationship was not a symbolic one but a literal and total one. They had "bet their whole lives" on what was going on between them and the departed spirits.

Insofar as I have been able to find, the Muslim religion, with its heavy emphasis upon monotheism, is more prone to interpret behavior in terms of idolatry than is either Hinduism or Buddhism. The Muslim likens an idolater to "the spider who buildeth her a house: but, verily, frailest of all houses surely is the house of the spider." (Quoted from the Koran by Edward Sell, "Images and Idols (Muslim)," in James Hastings, ed., *Encyclopedia of Religion and Ethics,* Vol. VII, p. 150; Charles Scribner's Sons, 1928.) To the Muslim, idolatry is the unpardonable sin. Yet Hinduism and Buddhism alike are more syncretistic religions and permit polytheistic worship of nature, veneration of ancestors, etc. This "lower" type of worship for the populace rarely reaches the level of conferring ultimate significance upon the object of worship. The objects of worship do not become matters of total identification of the finite with the infinite.

PSYCHOLOGICAL ESTIMATES OF ULTIMATE AND PROXIMATE RELIGIOUS CONCERN

Several psychologists have been definitive about the mature religious sentiment, as Gordon Allport calls it.

By negative reference, the sick religious concern can be pointed out. Allport speaks of religious concern in terms of *interest, outlook,* or a *system of beliefs.* This is a system of readiness that we use in coping with life. When thought and feeling are organized and directed toward some highly chosen object of value—a mother, a son, a neighborhood, a nation, or a church—"we call the system a sentiment." Then Allport defines a specifically religious sentiment by saying that it is *"a disposition, built up through experience, to respond favorably, and in certain habitual ways to conceptual objects and principles that the individual regards as of ultimate importance in his own life, and as having to do with what he regards as permanent or central in the nature of things"* (italics his). This allows for a wide variety of religious expressions, but it gives a good inner view of how the individual with the religious sentiment feels about it.

Then Allport continues to identify the characteristics of a religious sentiment. It has a well-differentiated *capacity of self-criticism.* As Anton Boisen used to say, the mature prophet has a certain consciousness of "prophesying in part," a genuine humility. Sick religion, correspondingly, is uncritical, self-contained, and lacks any measure of humility and teachableness. In the second place, the *dynamic character* of a religious sentiment provides the main index to its health or unhealth. Immature religion is shot through with magical thinking, self-justification, and personal comfort. Mature religion is the master in the economy of life, controlling motives rather than being controlled and determined by them. The control is directed toward a goal "that is no longer determined by mere self-interest." In the third place, a mature religious sentiment is characterized by a *consistency of moral consequences of the religion itself.* The criterion of moral consistency suggests that the mature religious sentiment generates high and consistent standards of action. This speaks to the religious sociopath's situation, wherein religion becomes a *means* of immoral behavior of various kinds. (Gordon Allport, *The Individual and His Religion,* pp. 56 ff.; The Macmillan Company, 1950.)

The focus of this chapter on the idolatrous character of sick religion, however, is clarified best by Allport's assertion that a mature religious sentiment is a *comprehensive* sentiment. A nonidolatrous kind of religion calls for a comprehensive philosophy of life. The Hindus said that "truth is one and men call it by many names." Plato said that sin is the rising up of a part of the soul against the whole. The Hebrew prophets and the Lord Jesus Christ insisted that we cannot serve two masters but that purity of heart calls for a Lord of lords. A comprehensive faith embraces the whole order of creation. The idol is a "part-process," a restriction and constriction of the life. The negative counterpart of this comprehensive religious sentiment is what Andras Angyal calls the domination of the whole sphere of life by a "part-process," which thrusts the organism into a state of "bionegativity." In the illness, whether it be of a psychotic order or a behavioral disorder, the identity of the person takes on a negative character instead of a positive and constructive nature.

The previous examples of the restriction of life around the spirits of the departed dead make Allport's point of view more concrete. However, we need more precise clinical demonstration of the way in which life is constricted and controlled through the worship of something less than the Eternal. Bereavement, preoccupation with the family inheritance, and preoccupation with one role in life to the exclusion of all others provide three areas where the point of view set forth here can be demonstrated clinically.

THREE AREAS OF CONSTRICTION

Bereavement

Lindemann, Wallis, and others have established through empirical studies the validity of interpreting grief as a process with varying but definable stages. The loss of someone by death moves through the stages of shock, numbness, a struggle with reality as over against fantasy, a time of depression and a flood of tears, a re-grouping of the life with sporadic bursts of memory reac-tivating the previous stages momentarily, and finally a reordering of the whole life around new interests, rela-tionships, and pursuits in life. Pathologically, the person may become arrested in the process of grief at the stage of shock, numbness, or the struggle with fantasy, or at the time of depression. The loss of someone by death can, therefore, be a precipitating factor in severe emotional disorders of various kinds, depending upon the life history and style of life of the person. The religious life of the person quite regularly becomes the first casualty in his life and may take on all of the symptomatology of sick religion. Various sources of data can be consulted here.

Comparative studies between a primitive religion and psychotic episodes among people in a technological society are productive of insights as to how very thin the veneer of our so-called Western civilization really is. J. H. M. Beattie offers a clinical study of the relation between belief-reactions to the spirit of someone who has died and illness among the Bunyoro. He carried out these field studies in Bunyoro, Uganda, for about twenty-two months, during 1951 through 1953 and in 1955. He developed case history details on fifteen individuals whose illnesses were attributed to the ghosts of the departed dead. Of the fifteen cases, three were epilepsy, five were miscarriages, one was a sudden seizure, one was an undiagnosed fatal illness, one was leprosy, one was a painful swelling, one was an allergy to certain foods, one was ulcers on the legs, and one was a man who set fire to some property.

However, the most interesting fact about these involvements with the dead was that "in eight out of the fifteen cases . . . where ghostly activity was diagnosed, the original offender was not attacked directly but through his children, and in two others he was long since dead and vengeance was wreaked upon his descendants." (J. H. M. Beattie, "The Ghost Cult in Bunyoro," in John Middleton, ed., *Gods and Rituals: Readings in Religious Beliefs and Practices,* pp. 259–261; The Natural History Press, 1967.) The important thing for the reader to note is that bereavement is ordinarily associated in the Western mind with the death of someone, but the technical distinction I am making is that a person may be *alienated* from a living person and suffer a more profound grief reaction than if that person had died. Death is definitive and can be identified easily. A hostile separation is not so easy to grasp. For example, the Bunyoros substituted an innocent living person for a deceased individual who had offended someone. In contemporary psychotic behavior, the substitution of an innocent person for one's own offenses, the offenses of other living persons, or the offenses of deceased persons appears as a distortion of moral responsibility. For another example:

Mr. Daily was a twenty-one-year-old man admitted to the hospital with terrible feelings of having committed an awful and unpardonable sin that he could not identify. He was referred to the hospital from a remote rural region by an area missionary. His father was a lay preacher, and his mother a housewife. He had two sisters, one eleven and one seventeen. He felt that his father was always on his back and that he gave preference at all times to the sisters. The patient had had two years of college and had taught in a rural county school for one year. He felt much anxiety over his "call" to be a minister, but daydreamed considerably about other roles in life—being a missionary bachelor, being a policeman, etc.

There had been no previous illnesses of a psychiatric nature. The presenting symptoms at this time were sleeplessness, and a strong feeling that he had sinned against God and that God was going to punish his younger sister for his sins. He was worried deeply about the safety and well-being of this sister. As he underwent treatment, both chemotherapy and electroconvulsive therapy, this fear for his younger sister's safety went away, but it returned in the form of a similar fear about the safety of the older sister. He could express his anger at God for punishing someone like his sisters, who were suffering for things he himself had done.

During the course of treatment, the concerns about his sisters became less compulsive and obsessive. He could think of them in the past tense. As he did so, the focus of

his anger shifted from God to a frank acceptance of negative and destructive feelings toward his father. Upon
entry into the hospital he had extolled his father's great
kindness to him and his perfect instruction of him in
salvation from God. Upon outpatient treatment, he was
able to express some of his anger toward his father, who
had "restricted him too much," to use his own words.

The father himself also felt that he had forced his son
to lead too sheltered a life and that he had not wanted to
let him be anything except his "little boy."

The conception of God in this account is a "ghostly"
one. God is seen as a ghost to be feared. Also, he is seen
as one who unjustly punishes someone whom we love and
"gets at us" through them. Of course, the anger is really
Mr. Daily's in this case, and the vengeful mood is his
own toward his favored sisters. The "ghost god" is a vehi-
cle of his own anger toward his sisters and toward his
father for treating them with favoritism.

After dialogue with the patient, I met a private psychiatrist who said that within the last twenty-four hours
he had met two patients. One of them had lost her
mother by death about ten months previously. The other
had given birth to a badly malformed child. Each said
similar things of God: "God will punish you. He will get
at you by hurting the person closest to you!" Here in
these instances cited by the psychiatrist, grief was present
in the loss of someone by death as well as alienation from
someone by misunderstanding. In both instances, as in
the case of the psychotic patient, Mr. Daily, and in the
previous references to the Bunyoros, an innocent third
party is seen to be the victim.

The overlay of Christian symbols does not remove the

basically primitive character of the "ghost cult" within
the ranks of somewhat educated people. The patient en-
dows the fear of his own anger toward his parents and
siblings with ultimate concern. As such, his own uncon-
trolled impulses are the source of his "bondage" and distress. Not until he begins to recognize his own feelings
and accept limitation upon them can he begin to function
effectively and happily.

No specific bereavement caused by death provided the
"ghost" in the case of Mr. Daily. The bereavement was
due to the breach between the patient and his father.
If the father had died, the situation would be synonymous
with that of the Bunyoro tribe. The young man's father
was not dead. God, instead, became the ghost between
father and son, working punishment on the patient by
threatening his sisters. The combined erotic and hostile
impulses toward the sisters made the overwhelming fear
a compound of guilt and anxiety of pathological propor-
tion. A "ghostly" conception of God took the persecutor's
role.

The Japanese religions are different from modern
Judeo-Christian faiths at the point of the custom of worshiping the dead. At one and the same time, the transla-
tion of a loved one into an ancestor lowers the reality of
death and makes the separation anxiety less severe than
in Western Christian tradition. Yamamato and his associates studied twenty widows who were the bereaved wives
of traffic accident victims. Eighteen of the twenty had
either Buddhist or Shinto family altars (butsudan) in
their homes. Yamamato compared his and his associates'
results with those of a London psychiatrist, C. M. Parkes.
They discovered that the Japanese widows suffered signi-

ficantly less depression, numbness and apathy, sleeplessness, and cultivation of and the actual sense of the presence of the dead than did the London group of widows.
In turn, the London widows had significantly more awareness of the presence of the dead, trouble escaping re-
minders of the dead, and difficulty in accepting the loss of
the deceased. One would ask whether or not the encouragement of ancestor reverence does not lower the psychic
stress at the expense of a more realistic handling of the
harsher reality of death. Yet the cultural affirmations of
ancestor reverence among the Japanese might well lower
the incidence of mental illness with grief as a precipitating factor. (Joe Yamamato, M.D., Keigo Ogonogi, M.D.,
Tetsuya Iwasahi, M.D., and Saburo Yoshimura, M.D.,
"Mourning in Japan," *American Journal of Psychiatry,* Vol. 125, No. 12, June, 1969, pp. 1660–1665.)

The Inheritance Syndrome

The family inheritance is another common repository
of the ultimate concern of a person. In turn, the family
inheritance becomes an idol constricting the life of the
individual. The form and shape of this constriction often
derives its power and community sanction from religious
sources. Especially is this true when the life of the sick
person has been religious.

The story of the rich fool, found in Luke 12:13–21 of
the New Testament, exemplifies this situation. A man
came to Jesus asking that he make his brother divide the
family inheritance with him. Jesus refused the role of
divider and judge over him. Then he told the story of
the rich fool who gave himself entirely and solely to
the finite task of building a bigger and bigger estate. The

man's life was required of him in the process. Jesus asked, "Then whose will those things be?" It was a rhetorical question the answer to which was obvious: These things would be the sons' to argue over, to shape their lives by.

Jesus said to another man (as recorded in Luke 9:59), "Follow me." But he said, "Lord, let me first go and bury my father." The father may or may not have been at the point of death at that time. The family fortune, a mistaken sense of loyalty to a reasonably healthy parent, and an ultimate concern for the inheritance may have bound the son against following the Lord to whom he gave lip service. Preoccupation with the family's future can become an obsession and a sick religion. The following case is significant at this point:

A thirty-two-year-old man was the younger of two sons. The father and mother had become parents of the two sons late in life because they had wanted to become financially secure before they had children. The two sons came within two years of each other and grew to young manhood as part of the family business. The elder of the two sons became a very religious person, contrary to the pattern of the family as a whole. Under the tutelage and with the encouragement of his church, he became a missionary in a rural section of the United States, even though he had been reared in a large city. He stayed with the mission work faithfully and was gradually promoted in his duties until he became an editor of one of his church's publications. He established himself in his own right all the way across the continental United States apart from his father's business.

The younger son tried the same method of breaking away from the family business but failed. Each time he would try to establish himself in the work of the church, he would become emotionally sick and have to return home. His reasoning was that someone had to look after his aging father as long as he lived. But when faced with the realistic job of putting up with his father's eccentricities and the demands of the family business, he would become anxiously depressed and even suicidal. Upon admission to the hospital for treatment he would say: "If I could only be a missionary like my brother, I wouldn't be sick. It is all due to my unfaithfulness to God." But underneath this, there was his quiet assurance that if he waited long enough, the inheritance would be his and he would not have to worry. As he became less depressed and expressed his hopes about life, this was the way he reassured himself. Realistic plans for him to learn a kind of work of "his own" apart from both his brother and his father ran aground upon his settled assurance that when he buried his father, his troubles would be over because the inheritance would be his. The task of therapy was to challenge and change this settled resolve of the patient at the same time that the symptoms of depression, anxiety, and suicidal indications were managed therapeutically.

The course of treatment involved intensive social-work efforts to devise a fitting kind of meaningful work in which the man could use his skills as a salesman apart from the sales organization of his father. He also needed his own identity apart from the missionary position of his brother. The pastoral counselor was in the position of collaborating with the patient to find the approval and acceptance of God for the work the patient decided he realistically should do "under God." When the clutching fingers of his devotion to the family fortune—little in fact that it was—loosened, the man became less sentimental about his father, less depressed about his own worthlessness, and more confident of his own future in a sales job for which he was both talented and fitted.

In summary, the "part-process" of preoccupation over an inheritance dominated and possessed the total life of the persons described. The inheritance takes on an ultimate significance for the person who permits it to become the total direction of his life. As subtle and somewhat nebulous as this may be, it becomes much clearer when we see the inheritance as an idolatrous construction of the individuals involved. In sentimental concern over the well-being of the father or mother whose path is presupposed if the inheritance is to be received, the person builds a reaction formation to mask his guilt at the wish for the death of the parent.

Self-reflection

The most malignant form of religious sickness probably comes from a perfectionistic expectation of oneself as a self. The classic statement of this is Nietzsche's exclamation: "There is no God! If there were, how could I stand it if I were not he?" Caught between the necessity of his humanity and the possibility of his divinity, a person settles the tension between the two on the side of his infinitude. As Kierkegaard, who set forth this paradox most clearly in his *Sickness Unto Death*, says, a person becomes "drunk on infinitude." The following case history is illustrative:

An eighteen-year-old girl attempted suicide at the college where she was a freshman. She was sufficiently dangerous to herself for the college authorities to advise her parents to have her hospitalized. During her hospital stay she repeatedly threatened to try suicide again.

Her family history revealed a father who worked as a day laborer, a mother who served as a maid, a brother in the Armed Services, and the patient herself the youngest daughter. She was the only one of her family who went beyond the sixth grade and her church has made her college education possible at a church-related college. Her father was hostile toward her getting so much education. Her mother silently approved it but gave little or no verbal encouragement to the strivings of the girl toward an education.

The minister of the patient had been very influential in her life, convincing her that she could do excellent work and that there was no limit to her possibilities as a student. She despaired at reaching his expectations, but used her assurance from him as a way of "putting down" her father. This patient vacillated between exceptional elation and unremitting despair.

When I was introduced to her by a nurse, the girl's first remark to me was an elated, "What can I do for you?" She spoke of her homesickness, but shifted quickly to discussing her service in a teaching project for underprivileged children. She could not get over the betrayal she felt at being shipped by her school to a hospital, and consoled herself by saying that she must now decide alone what she was to do with her life. She talked frankly about killing herself as a way of "hating my parents and the school to death." Suicide was one way of getting out from under the tyranny of her expectations of herself and at the same time of getting back at those she held responsible for her plight.

One conversation pinpoints the crucial issue of her deification of her own self-expectations. In this third conversation, Miss———talked about what she said was "really wrong" with her. She said:

"I've tried to be God and I've expected other people to

be God. When I couldn't make it, nothing was worth anything. If I could not be God, I didn't want to be anything. When I was in high school I won all the honors and did not expect to do so. I was surprised, but when I got to college, I thought there was nothing I couldn't do. Then I turned up with above-average grades but not perfect ones. This destroyed me.

"I also had a minister who I thought was a god. He could do no wrong. He was everything—savior, lover, everything—to me. Then when I didn't do as well as he expected me to, he just cut me off. He led me to believe that my intelligence was so great that I could do anything. When I didn't make it, he just cut me off."

She said: "I didn't want to be human. That is not good enough." We talked about the courage it takes to be neither less than nor more than human. It was a thorough discussion of the "importance of being human."

The crucial issue in this chapter is twofold: the true nature of the Eternal and the acceptance of the limitations of our humanity. The problem is far more than that of accepting ourselves as sinners in the face of forgiveness. This is a problem we shall discuss in a later chapter. The problem of the idolatry of the self is that of accepting ourselves as human—limited in power, in time, in space, in everything. When these limits are denied and rejected, whatever forms of religion we have become sick. Religion becomes a tool of our basic rejection of our human condition.

PASTORAL APPROACHES

The pastoral care of a person bound to a loyalty less than God is not one of harshness. When the finite powers an individual has trusted fail him, he is likely to become religiously sick if he has taken religion at all seriously in the first place. As a result, he is shattered along with the confidence he has placed in the idol that possesses him. A shattered person does not need further shattering. What does he need?

Comfort and Catharsis

The first prerequisite of a pastoral relationship is that of the pastor's taking the role of a comforter in the face of the disillusionment brought about by the collapse of the idol. The twenty-one-year-old young man who feared for the safety of his sisters was suffering from a collapse of his hopes that his father would *ever* come to his senses and bring some degree of encouragement to him as the firstborn, a son with a birthright that was denied him in the preoccupation of the father with the sisters. The son felt permanently denied a place of his own in the family. The objective of pastoral care of the young man was to establish a relationship in which there would be an absence of competition and to give him individual attention. This provided a comfort that was more than superficial "cheerleader"-type words. The importance of fixed times for visits gave the patient points in time to which he could look forward. The experiences of life had unhinged the patient's orientation to time, work, play, and sleep. Medication and electroconvulsive treatments were employed by the physicians to restore these. Psychotherapy was instituted by the physician after the ECT was concluded. Reeducating the parents and creating the opportunity for completing college were the tasks of the social workers. The task of the pastoral counselor was that of giving his undivided attention and comfort to the patient as these other therapies took place, plus allowing the patient opportunity to feel free to pour out his complaint to God. The infinite God was portrayed as one who can hear with affection the darkest feelings we have to express.

Thus a catharsis of the patient's feelings of disillusionment, injustice, and disappointment could be expressed. Also, he confessed that the illness itself was pleasant in that this way he could really be "Daddy's little boy" and have first place in Daddy's attention. Such confession and subsequent insight comes only through disciplined listening that enables a person to speak his or her most private thoughts without fear of pastoral probing.

Confrontation of the Constricting Powers of Idols

When patients are convalescing from an acute psychotic episode, they, like surgical patients, tend to want to "sort out" what happened to them, how they feel about the past, their treatment, and the future. At this time, *if the pastor has had an effective and faithful relationship with the patient during the episode,* he has an opportunity to philosophize with him about the nature of his primary concerns in life. The pastor runs the hazard of just replacing the idols of the past with an idolatry of himself. Both this possibility and previous constrictions on the life of the patient can be challenged and confronted. This the pastor is in a position to do during the rebuilding of the realistic confidence of a patient during convalescence.

For example, the young man who was waiting for his father's inheritance to be his was confronted very frankly with the fact that his aging father would indeed die sooner or later. Decision on the son's part now toward becoming self-sustaining in his own right could not but make for more self-confidence when the father's death did take place. Just to sit and wait for someone to die drains the present of meaning and casts a shadow on the hopes one has for the future. Encouragement of each move toward the patient's effective mastery of his own job was part of the positive reinforcement of a nonidolatrous kind of functioning. As Rudolf Dreikurs has said: *"Deficiencies are not eliminated by being emphasized.* One cannot build on weaknesses, only on strengths." The process of encouragement is more than kindness; it is constructive reinforcement of the strongest and most positive intentions of the person as a whole. (Rudolf Dreikurs, M.D., *Psychology in the Classroom,* 2d ed., p. 97; Harper & Row, Publishers, Inc., 1968.) In Judeo-Christian values, encouragement—according to Chaplain Myron Madden—is the power to bless, to invest belief in a person in such a way that the person feels it to be genuine.

Therefore, the pastoral challenge is to discover with the person the real strengths of his life and to concentrate on these, not his deficiencies. Real strengths are an individual's direct contact with his true self and with a nonidolatrous loyalty in life.

Frank Discussion of the Nature of God

The minister's primary responsibility is to know God and to speak frankly and without glibness of him. Working with the religiously sick focuses this responsibility. I recall a seminar with a group of senior psychiatric residents at an Eastern Seaboard hospital. The first question was asked by a young Hindu resident. He said, "What is it that you do in relation to a patient that a psychiatrist

does not do?" I replied: "I, when I am introduced to the
patient as a pastor or a minister, always represent God.
The psychiatrist may occasionally do this by choice, but
the minister does so of necessity when he is presented or
presents himself as a minister." "But," replied the Hindu
doctor, *"which* God do you represent? There are many."
I replied: "The God I represent to the patient is the
patient's God, and there *are* many. My first task is to
discover who and of what nature is his God." The Hindu
physician pressed further, "But what is *your* God like?"
I replied: "My God is like Jesus of Nazareth, but this does
not mean that I can assume that everyone else's God is the
same as my own. These differences are the stuff of our
conversation. I will learn as well as will the person with
whom I converse."

Frank discussion of the nature of God is a part of the
later phases of a patient's care by a minister. The bene-
ficent restoration to a reasonable pattern of conversation
is the end intention and desired result of intensive
psychiatric treatment. The restortion of a rational,
realistic perception is one of the healing results of psychiatric treatment. As one doctor said, "The doctor's job is to
help people see straight, and the minister's job is to see
to it that they are looking at the right God when they
seek to be religious."

For example, the suicidal patient mentioned above,
when faced with the possibility of leaving the hospital,
became apprehensive about whether she would attempt
suicide again. She said: "I am trapped. I don't want to
return home and I don't want to stay here. Suicide seems
the only way out. I wonder if God can forgive me for what
I have done and am thinking about doing." When asked,

"*Which* God is that?" she replied, "The Almighty God."
I told her that this God could forgive her and enable her
to find other alternatives for living. I explained that the
god of her own need to be perfect could not be forgiving
the way the Almighty God can.

In a letter she wrote after her return home, she said:
"I'm finally on the road to recovery. I finally admitted to
myself and others why I wanted to die—actually I did not
want to die. I wanted someone to care and I needed to
change some things in my life and suicide offered 'the easy
way out.' "

Another patient, in speaking to a group of chaplains,
said: "Go easy on how you tell us that God cares. Show
us that you care and we'll decide for ourselves whether
God cares on the basis of what you do!"

IN SUMMARY

This chapter has emphasized the ways in which the substitution of a limited, finite loyalty for an ultimate, comprehensive concern is for all practical purposes a false
center of idolatry. This, in turn, produces a disturbed
balance in the whole life. Bereavement, preoccupation
over the family inheritance, and deification of the self as
perfect were chosen as clinical working models for demon-
strating the sickness of religion known as idolatry.
Specific pastoral approaches of conflict and catharsis, confrontation, and frank discussion of the nature of the God
of reality were described in some detail.

Chapter 3

SUPERSTITION,
MAGIC,
AND SICK RELIGION

IDOLATROUS CONSTRICTION leaves much of life unattended.
The "ghostly" gods of the dead, of the finite hopes of
inheritance, and of one's own imagination of his own
perfection leave untapped the possibility of an abundant
life for an individual. Life is wasted. One negative side
effect of such constriction is the development of a life of
superstition. The world becomes populated with omens,
signs, and other mysterious connections that control life.
In order to counter and manage these mysterious forces,
magic—incantations, rituals, and superstitious ways of
thinking—must be developed as antidotes. These magical
formulas, for all practical purposes, become a way of life.

When this process takes place within the culture of a
religion such as Judaism or Christianity, the forms of
these faiths that are most persuasive become the vehicles
of the feeling of fate. For example, the following case
material is illustrative of what I mean:

A forty-eight-year-old man was a devout and active
member of a Disciples of Christ Church. By occupation he
was a public school teacher. His wife was also a public
school teacher. Both of them held positions of leadership

in their church. They had made a vow when they were married that they would never have children. They did not want to perpetuate their two families' histories because neither of them was proud of the family that produced them. They were both "heredity buffs" and felt that heredity was *the* cause of much or most of human ills. They chose to devote themselves to teaching and church work rather than to have children of their own. The husband was a very dependent man and the wife was a very motherly person.

Their adjustment to life enabled them to accomplish much good in their small city community, and they gave of themselves liberally to the needs of other people. This worked quite well until they discovered that the wife was pregnant at the age of forty-seven. She brought the child to full term and delivered a beautiful baby girl.

They took separate approaches to the coming of the child. The wife and mother spent her full time in caring for the child, having quit her job and lost her interest in the work of the church. She was so absorbed in the care of the child that she more often than not had no meals prepared for her husband when he came home from work. They took separate bedrooms so that she could give full attention to the child at night without disturbing her husband's sleep.

The husband, in turn, redoubled his efforts in school work and church work. He sought to make up for the difference caused by his wife's loss of interest in the works of the community. He became intensely interested in studying theology with especial interest in the Second Coming of the Lord Jesus Christ. He began to doubt that he was a Christian at all and he sought reassurance from everyone that he had not committed "the unpardonable sin." He began to lose sleep and to refuse to eat until "Jesus comes." It was at this point that his pastor and his family physician sought psychiatric consultation and hospitalization for him.

This couple's situation represents not only a serious value upheaval occasioned by the advent of the child. As a couple, they represent the difficulty of reorganizing one's values at middle life when those values have already been established on unrealistic and even neurotic bases. The process of treatment took into consideration the necessity of psychotherapeutic reorganization of the goal structure of these persons' lives as well as their support as a family as they adjusted late in life to the radical event of child-bearing.

The symptomatology presented by the husband, however, is illustrative of the magical use of religion to ward off impending doom. Religion became a means of incantation of the sense of impending destruction the man felt. In a real sense, the world which he had constructed *had* come to an end. The underlying fear that compelled him was the fear that, inasmuch as his world had come to an end, he would kill himself. This *was* the unpardonable sin he feared committing. Facing this in a protected environment was a part of his recovery.

Superstitions and the magical use of religion can be valuable in the diagnosis of the disorders of the patient, according to Draper and his associates. They should not be brushed aside as insignificant. Neither should they be taken as an authentic representation of the validity or invalidity of the particular living religion whose symbols they use. Rather, they should be viewed as a sick use of the religion—a time when religion becomes sick. In other words, one of the times religion becomes sick is when the accidents, the uncontrollable events and the inevitable demands of life call for acceptance of changes and responses to growth that the individual cannot maneuver, manage, nor accept. He then resorts to placation of evil spirits, magical incantation of the "powers" that control the "shape of things to come," and develops elaborate explanations of his behavior in terms of the religious symbols he has been trained to use. The end result is what the behavior therapists call "odd behavior."

CHANCE AND ACCIDENTS IN A RELIGIOUS PERSON'S MIND

Underneath the patient's behavior is a world view that *all behavior* is determined totally by God, that there is no such thing as a chance of more than one outcome for any given situation, and that even within the variety of directions a course of events could take, there is no such thing as the fortuitous "break" of events in which accidents change the whole direction of a given history. William Pollard, the executive director of the Oak Ridge Institute of Nuclear Studies, says that "there are two sources of indeterminacy in history. One of these is chance." By this he means "the available alternative responses to a given set of causative influences." "Another source of indeterminism in history . . . is accident." He uses "accident" to refer to situations "in which two or more chains of events have no causal connection with each other. . . . The accidental does not depend on the presence of choice and alternative in natural phenomena." (William Pollard, *Chance and Providence,* pp. 73–74; Charles Scribner's Sons, 1958.)

At the core of superstition and its rituals of magic is the assumption of a hidden purpose, which we can determine if we will just perform the right act in the right way at the right time. Thus everything becomes controllable and every outcome is predictable; we can be secure because what is going to happen has been decided by our behavior. We have nothing to worry about now. The risks of the future have been charted, precautions taken, and we are safe.

As Lévy-Bruhl said of the primitive mentality much earlier: "Nothing ever happens by accident. What appears to us Europeans [and Americans] is, in reality, always the manifestation of a mystic power. . . . There is no such thing as chance to a mind like this, nor can there be. Not because it is convinced of the rigid determinism of phenomena . . . it remains indifferent to the relation of cause and effect and attributes a mystic origin to every event which makes an impression upon it." (Lucien Lévy-Bruhl, *Primitive Mentality,* p. 43; Beacon Press, Inc., 1966.)

My own basic premise is that among even sophisticated Americans exposed to the popular nuances of Judaism and Christianity, a subterranean flow of this same kind of superstition about mystic origins of events "indifferent to the relation of cause and effect" is at the heart of much sick religion, especially among the mentally ill. The rituals that are cautiously developed are seemingly sense-less. But they are calculated to take the risk, the unpredictable, and the unknown out of life.

Little wonder is it that prudential ethics have been built on cultural mores that are calculated to make us healthy, wealthy, and wise. As Paul Tillich has said, the risk element has been removed from a legalistic morality of safety. A morality of adventure calls for taking risks, the courage to move into the unknown. The prophetic faiths call for this element of risk and the capacity to absorb ambiguity and unpredictableness. Yet the religion of superstition and magic works to control and obliterate the unknown and the risky by the legalisms, the taboos, the rituals of incantation, and the obsessive acts that are developed as magical controls.

When we see the histories of mental patients from conception to maturity, we see even at the point of conception the variables of heredity. These are not nearly so predictable as we once thought. In the process of prenatal development, chance and accident coexist with predetermined course. In the development process after birth, the great transitions from one era to another are crises of necessity and possibility interacting with each other. Even in later years of maturity, cerebral changes take place that are the end result of chance, accident. They are seen even legally as "acts of God," when in reality they are not.

My hypothesis is that religion becomes sick when a person loads the whole responsibility for these "thrown situations" entirely upon God and thereby thrusts the whole responsibility for changing the situation upon him. Thus God becomes the ghostly visitant of all the thousand mortal ills the flesh is heir to. Patients' rituals are their efforts to placate the caprice of their god to change the situation. Into the mythology of this set of beliefs flows the flood of religious symptomatology we deal with in the religiously sick. Usually these patterns of religious behavior have been taught the person from infancy. The kind of religion described here was used as positive reinforcement of approved behaviors by parents, grandparents, pastors, and teachers. It was also used as taboo, punishment, and negative reinforcement of disapproved behaviors, ideas, and attitudes. Usually persons suffering from this kind of sick religion have been suffering so for a long time, and the demands of maturity have brought a chronic situation to crisis.

This forty-three-year-old woman is an assembly-line worker in an electronics company. She has a high school education plus one year of college. She is married to a man who is her own age, an auto mechanic, a veteran of World War II, and given to periodic times of drunkenness that interrupt his work and have at times resulted in his losing his job. They have no children, having lost their first and only child fourteen years prior by a premature birth. They live in a house for which they are paying, but the bills are paid from the wife's income. Both husband and wife are Protestant, but belong to different denominations. Hers is very strict concerning attendance at movies, dancing, drinking, and smoking; his is much more flexible about these things.

Presenting symptoms. In the patient's own words, she says: "I can be in church and get fearful, almost like I'm leaping over something—like I'm thinking or trying to think evil and bad thoughts. The first time it happened most severely was during the Lord's Supper. I was afraid to drink and afraid not to. I remembered what the Bible says about eating and drinking 'damnation' to yourself. I felt I would die before I got out of there if I did the wrong thing. I've felt this way at funerals and in church. I'm so afraid that I'll think a blasphemous thought, I get beside myself. I stay depressed for days, crying much of the time.

"If it is Satan, I know the Lord will see me through. When I'm tempted, I use affirmations of Scriptures and hymns, but Satan even attacks me through them. I say to myself: 'Do this!' Is this a premonition or mental telepathy or something? I've been doing it for years."

The longer term history. For three years after her birth the patient lived with her parents. She has one younger sister. The mother divorced the father because of alcoholism when the patient was three. Each parent went to his parental home, taking one of the children for the grandparents to raise. The patient went with the father to the paternal grandparents. The grandmother was in her sixties, a very, very religious woman, and used religious beliefs about the end of the world, the displeasure of God, and the ever presence of the devil as a means of disciplining the patient as a child. As the patient became older, she worked and prepared all year round for excellence in the youth activities of her church. She joined the church when she was nine years of age. She says: "During this time I read my Bible but would be frightened by the thoughts of 'before' and 'after' time. I made myself afraid with the thought that the world would end. I would become afraid when I read the book of Revelation.

"I lost time in school (nearly two years) for being too nervous to go. Measles, mumps, whooping cough, and bronchitis were all mine. I remember little of this except a sign in the doctor's office that read:

Go nowhere you wouldn't want to be found when Jesus comes;

Say nothing you wouldn't want to be saying when Jesus comes;

Do nothing you wouldn't want to be doing when Jesus comes.

"I finished high school and married two years later. A year later we lost our little girl because she was premature and because of my unbelief. I always thought the world would end before I had any children. We still don't have any. My sin."

This patient has made repeated professions of faith in revival meetings she has attended. She struggles with cursing thoughts against God, thoughts like those her husband expresses in his drunken rages.

She refuses to be critical of her husband, to face the possibility of her marriage breaking up, or to come to grips in face-to-face discussion with him about the painful aspects of their relationship. She denies problems of a causal nature arising out of the habitual patterns of discipline set by her grandmother, or those arising out of her feelings of injustice in relation to her husband. Instead, she seeks more and more religious rituals, reassurances, and ruminations to ward off the fears that beset her.

The program of treatment. This patient was hospitalized for a period of three months. Chemotherapy, electroconvulsive therapy, and subsequent psychotherapy were used during her hospitalization. She was involved in social group therapy and learned to participate in many recreations she would have refused in her natural habitat—dancing, playing cards, movie attendance, etc. She never expressed negative emotions except through the "nuisance value" of her repetitive religious ideas. To the contrary, she was unusually sweet and protested forcefully that she "loved" all people. Yet she despised and loathed herself as unworthy of man's or God's approval. She was seen regularly by a pastoral counselor during hospitalization.

The patient was dismissed with a guarded prognosis and a plan for continued contact. She was improved to the extent that she could do her work without difficulty.

The follow-up history. A plan was established for the patient to see a pastoral counselor in her neighborhood on a regular and formal basis. This relationship became a regular emotional nutriment to this deprived person over a period of five years. The pastoral counselor was in constant contact with her family physician, who supervised medication for the patient.

In her spare time, the patient started back to college with her husband's full support and consent. She received her college degree and took a job as an apprentice in a social welfare agency. She continued her religious interest but found attendance at most churches a burden to her. She listened to TV religious programs but was made fearful, sleepless, and apprehensive by going to church.

A second major episode in her illness occurred when the pastoral counselor to whom she had regularly gone left the area. This was concurrent in time with her medical doctor's advice that she have a complete hysterectomy. She was so agitated that she was referred to a nearby psychiatrist for psychotherapy and returned to this author for pastoral guidance and consultation. She successfully underwent the surgery and yet not without a heavy recurrence of her religious preoccupation. This went somewhat as indicated in her own words in the above account. The precise habits of thinking were repeated almost verbatim. The most significant addition was: "You should see how well I can take antidepressants and cry at the same time. If crying could heal, I'd have been well long ago for I've cried a river. Also, I'm still plagued by the idea that not going to church is turning from Christ, which I don't want to do. At the same time, I have the feeling that just going to church is just trying to be 'religious.' . . . I used to use magic to keep things from happening that I didn't think I could cope with. I wouldn't talk of things that scared or upset me for fear they would happen."

The patterns of treatment that have been used with this patient over a period of six years have been unevenly effective. Her molds of thinking and behaving remain existentially the same—unhappy, inwardly torn, and fearful in relationships. Her basic function as a worker in production lines and in school has been even except during the two periods of hospitalization, one for a depression and the other for the gynecologic surgery. The most recent episode was intimately related to the coincidence of both the menopause and the need for a hysterectomy.

Yet the religious sickness, consisting of a "ghostly" conception of God, elaborate religious mythologies of the end of the world, and a confessed feeling of need for magical practices to ward off evil, remains essentially unchanged in spite of extensive pastoral counseling by the author and another trained pastoral counselor.

END-SETTING OR TRANSFUSIONS OF EGO STRENGTH

Gerda E. Allison, M.D., reports the case of a thirty-five-year-old woman who was reared by an extremely demanding, controlling, and perfectionistic mother and a father who submitted to the mother's controls in every way except in his pursuit of a very fundamentalistic religion. The patient's mother died when the patient was twenty-five and she and the father developed a very close dependency upon each other. The patient refused marriage to a young doctor because the suitor would not "go along" with her own and her father's strict religious beliefs. Then, while the patient was away on a special teaching assignment, the father rather suddenly married without conferring with his daughter about it. He died of tuberculosis about three months later. At this time the patient became anxious and depressed. She sought psychiatric help. As to treatment, Dr. Allison says that he did not attempt to deal with the underlying dynamic material. Rather he used supportive therapy and encouraged her to express "her negative feelings toward God and her father in a rather oblique manner." He enabled her to build up her defenses and this allowed her to continue functioning in her work as a "conscientious but somewhat rigid head nurse." He says that she has maintained community with her religious group where she attends revivals, "where she obtains regular transfusions of ego strength." (Gerda E. Allison, M.D., "Psychiatric Implications of Religious Conversion," *Canadian Psychiatric Association Journal*, Vol. 12, 1967, pp. 57–58.)

There is an indirect evaluation of the revival here as a source of ego strength. I have observed this to be true in some instances and I am glad to have this confirmed by an unbiased observer. However, in the instance of the patient whose case is reported from my files, this was not true. She received her transfusions of ego strength from counseling sessions with a pastor. Yet in both instances, when we speak of this condition of replenishment of the ego that has from early childhood been deprived and rejected through the use of religious symbols, we may be confessing that there is such a thing as permanent emotional handicap that can be offset by such "transfusions of ego strength." We are not involved here in *curing* a patient, but in making a handicapped person useful to himself and other people.

A second case, that of a twenty-year-old patient, demonstrates the interaction of superstition, magic, and sick religion in the life of a man and his family.

For two years the man had been under psychotherapeutic outpatient treatment for phobic behaviors about eating, driving a car alone, and other fears clustering around his master fear of dying. He found that if he did not carry through his magical rituals, God would "zap" him, strike him dead.

A psychiatrist and a pastoral counselor treated him as cotherapists upon referral to them from a pastoral counselor and a psychiatrist in another state when the man changed his residence. The two professional persons in that state had not seen the patient at the same time. The magical rituals were, in effect, declared off limits for discussion. The superstitious character of the religious ideation was identified as superstition, not true religion. The basic vocational, marital, and realistic religious issues in the man's life situation were then confronted by the patient with psychiatrist and minister together in the same interview situation.

End-setting procedures were inherent in the time situation itself and the patient was not allowed to adopt "treatment" as a way of life. Rather, decisions were expected of him. His wife was involved in the treatment situation and was cooperative in the process. Life decisions were reviewed at an adult level under supervision. In the course of thirty interviews a new "life space" was discovered that gave both the man and his wife breathing room. The symptoms diminished in their intensity and number. In times of uncertainty they were reassessed by the patient as memories rather than as present events. When a crisis would come, the symptoms would reactivate until the crisis was past and then they would fall into the realm of memory again.

The value of joint therapy by minister and psychiatrist stands out as a plus feature of this second case. The value of an implosive "breakthrough" of the "odd behaviors" as magical rituals for a basically superstitious person and not as objects for continuous rumination even in psychotherapeutic interviews was evident in the case, at least. The value of time-limiting of the therapeutic process, lest the "game" of psychiatry or religion—as the case might be —became a substitute for life itself, was more than validated. Possibly, when defenses such as these phobias are needed periodically, they will recur, but, hopefully, the man will have a context for identifying them as magic, superstition, and sick religion—not as bona fide excuses from facing life and developing a life of faith as healthy religion.

The first case was dealt with through transfusions of ego strength. The second was focused upon an end-setting procedure. The question arises as to the relation between these two therapeutic approaches. One differentiating factor was that the diagnostic picture was different. In the case where end-setting procedures were used, the patient was primarily paranoid when he was emotionally disabled. Transfusions of ego strength were acceptable to the depressed patient, but very threatening to the paranoid patient. Other factors were drawn from the patients' developmental history. The one patient who was depressed had been rejected and deprived in her early life. The other patient had been pampered and overindulged in his earlier life. In the first patient, feelings of helplessness and powerlessness were stimulated by fears, magical feelings, and superstition. In the other, the manipulative cleverness of the patient was stimulated by similar fears, feelings, and superstitions. The one experienced feelings of worthlessness and the other experienced feelings of limitlessness and omnipotence. These were some of the bases of importance in making the decision between end-setting and transfusions of ego strength. A final one was the presence or absence of the suicidal possibility. End-setting procedures would be risky indeed with a person who was potentially suicidal.

CASE STUDIES OF
MAGIC, SUPERSTITION, AND RELIGIOUS HEALING

Records of the "magical response to superstition" expressions of sick religion have been recorded in some of the journal literature. Extensive studies of magic, faith, and healing have been published by psychiatrists who work in cross-cultural contexts and have to relate themselves to primitive attempts at psychotherapy, folk psychiatry, and contemporary American uses of persuasion in healing.

Most of these studies refer to the inclusion of primitive religious ideas and practices in the life pattern of persons of cultural and/or racial minorities in a technological society. For example, Ari Kiev studied the delusions of ten West Indian schizophrenics in English mental hospitals and found religious and magical themes that were taken from the layers of fundamentalist use of the Bible and ghost cults from their West Indian backgrounds. (Ari Kiev, "Beliefs and Delusions Among West Indian Immigrants to London," *British Journal of Psychiatry*, Vol. 109, 1963, pp. 356–363.)

With the movement of Southern rural Negroes into industries in Northern cities such as Rochester, New York, and Chicago, patients have been observed to use the "root work" of their primitive, self-help magic to allay the anxiety and despair associated with illness.

In nine cases of criminally convicted but apparently

psychotic Negro patients from the Bedford-Stuyvesant area of New York City, Bromberg and Simon found—with the work of Negro psychiatrists—an overlay of "to be expected" psychotic material: delusions, illusions, grandiosity, mannerisms, etc. But underneath these were somewhat coherent evidences of a thoroughgoing break with the patients' upbringing, with the Caucasian values of their general milieu, etc. These expressed themselves in "identification with the Islamic religion, fragments of voodoo practices, and an outright avowal of the Yaruba religion. What appears to be grandiosity and paranoid coloring of the productions of these patients derives directly from the 'primitive' religions and ideologies which function as a protest against centuries of domination by Caucasian values . . . the ego has not undergone sufficient impairment to justify a diagnosis of psychosis." (Walter Bromberg, M.D., and Frank Simon, M.D., "The Protest Psychosis: A Special Type of Reactive Psychosis," *Archives of General Psychiatry*, Vol. 19, No. 2, Aug., 1968, pp. 155–160.)

The objectivity required to study magical and superstitious uses of a living religion by exponents of that religion itself is almost if not entirely nonexistent. The following autobiographical account is an example of the way in which superstition can saturate the symbols of a living religion, issue in magical counteractions on the part of the person, and result in a pathological religious orientation to life. This woman spent three months in a mental hospital:

Being a young, Christian, blood-washed, redeemed, Child of God of nine months, I was not content to grow in the knowledge and grace of the Lord. I had the desire to run headlong down the narrow path and it almost led to my spiritual destruction mentally. Through not relying on the promises of God in His inspired Word, the Bible, I was willingly led (through demon possession of the mind) to an entirely new and different church group, entirely new as of the last fifty or so odd years as a supposed church. I had never doubted my salvation because I was completely delivered from alcohol even as far as the desire, proving that when the Lord Jesus does a thing, He does it right.

However, Satan, whom I found out I was no match for, knew that Jesus had taken over my heart, and there was no room for the devil, so he tormented me with all kinds of little things in my mind, thus robbing me of the joy of my salvation mentally. Because of my convinced knowledge, based on the promises of God's Word, that once saved always saved, and that God is not slack concerning His promises to a child of God, washed in the blood and covered by the blood, and that eternal life is a GIFT from God, and that God is not an Indian giver, but the Almighty Giver of life everlasting, I became overconfident, using my salvation as a crutch, with the idea that I couldn't really do anything that was wrong, because Jesus was my Savior and I knew it.

It was when I had gotten to that state that I started to walk by feet and not by faith. So these demons convinced me that I still didn't have a full experience with the Lord God. Thus I followed the direction in which these seducing spirits of Satan were pulling me. When inside this so-called church building, the power and friction in the air was terrific. This convinced me only more that I was led to the right place, and by the *Holy* Spirit yet! Then the call was given for anyone who had a testimony for the Lord. I was nervous and shaking inside; nevertheless, I stood up facing the congregation and said, "Jesus is the way and the truth and the life, and I know He is because I know," and then is when it happened.

I was filled with an ice cold air and I was froze (as it were) on my feet with my mouth open. This air came from the direction of the altar, and I was so numb that I couldn't sit down for at least three minutes. I just couldn't understand this, because I had so much to testify about my Lord Jesus. When I questioned others after the service they told me that it was an experience with the Lord, and that He was trying to reveal something to me, and that I must search the Scriptures to find out the answer, they couldn't tell me. They also said that this meant that I was close with the Lord and that He more fully wanted to use me as a servant and give me a gift. Now I was really confused, which is exactly what Satan had planned to do.

Now even though these demons were trying to absolutely convince me of the realness of this thing, Jesus was tugging at my heart because he knew I didn't know exactly what I was doing, yet I still had my own will, and he wasn't going to force me into coming out from among them. What a war was going on inside my mind for the space of two weeks. At home I walked around like I didn't know what I was doing and I was beginning to greatly fear as though I were some kind of criminal or something. It began to be noticeable [sic] to my friends. But do you know that those demons were so powerful, that they convinced them, through my mouth and out of curiosity [sic] to also go there to witness this thing. I almost denied my Lord Jesus, and caused others to do so too. Oh, how I have repented for my lack of faith, through willing ignorance. Satan made a fool out of me for his own sake, but Jesus has lifted me up again with his love through God the Father. He is truly Lord of Lords and King of Kings.

Satan had almost succeeded in planting a permanent seed of doubt in my mind with on-and-off-again salvation, trying to hold me in the bondage of fear. This type of religion so presents itself as the real thing that it is the perfect counterfeit of the day. I should rather have my feet cut off than to enter under the roof of any such establishment.

But now that I know this by the Grace of God, and especially that God is not the author of confusion and cannot lie, I will by the grace of God be content to grow.

These poor souls that are being used by Satan are in reality dedicated and sincere. But they are dedicated to Satan and sincerely wrong. I speak of them as poor souls because the Holy Spirit within me is grieved because of their willingness toward deception because even though they themselves are ignorant of the Truth, God will hold them accountable because there is no excuse.

These seducing spirits had taken over my mind and my members so much that I no longer even had control over my voice. The Scripture that came out of my mouth was true, but my voice deceived me. Outside I was a lamb, outside of the demon control, but inside I was a raving wolf. The way this was proven to me was by a Scriptural statement I made concerning the body, soul, and spirit, out loud in that demonic voice, which proved to be a WRONG statement. That was, I knew that it was no Holy Spirit voice.

Besides this evidence, that afternoon at home I became taut and tight inside all over and when I tried to relax, it just got worse. My mouth began to open slowly as by force until it was stretched open so far that I moaned with pain and called on Jesus, still not knowing what was going on. My hands seemed to get numb and rise slowly before me as if by force and I was so afraid that I hardly dared move at all. However, the worst part came when I tried reading the Scriptures aloud and laughed and talked real fast like a $33\frac{1}{3}$ r.p.m. record playing at 78 r.p.m. speed.

It was then that Satan told me I could heal myself of this fear and that the Lord had given me the gift of healing. I even believed this lie and looked around for some sore or abraised spot on my children. But after trying this I found that it did not work. I cried out to the Lord Jesus Christ in my agony of mind and it was then that He revealed to me that I was possessed with demons.

I was so blinded by these things (demons) in my mind that I didn't even know that I wasn't serving the only True God, and Savior Jesus Christ.

So now back to that assembly of people. I stood before the Pastor and his wife and told them these experiences and when I confessed with tears in my eyes that I was demon-possessed they just dropped their eyes and said that they would pray for me right there and then. Now they were under the impression that they were praying for my deliverance and it would happen then. Besides this they knew from all evidence that I had shown that I was that way, but yet I still was invited back all the time there, which would have made me one of those demons too.

But I thank the Lord Jesus, and I surely do, He knew my heart and when they cried out in prayer for me, it was to get rid of me. The proof was when instead of inviting me back another time, they gave me a calling card.

Yes, thank the Lord Jesus, He didn't want me back there any more either, but Satan still left his calling card. Now though, I through the Grace of God am reminded that I must call on Jesus and plead the blood by which I am covered when I am disturbed by tormenting thoughts and He alone will dismiss these demons from the mind. The awful lump in my throat was there because I would not cry out in true repentance and until I did it was not removed.

I say true repentance, never again to do that which I had done or was doing that kept me from close communion with my Savior.

This extensive autobiographical account calls for some explanatory observations to relate it to the discussion of magic, superstition, and sick religion. The reader will note that the obsessional preoccupation of the patient with "all kinds of little things" in her mind is attributed to the tormenting of the devil and is not seen in any sense as empirical cause and effect. Tactual feelings of power and friction in the air, being filled with ice cold air, the loss of control of the voice, numbness of the hands, etc., are described by the patient. The somatic involvements of religious experience weave themselves into a magical explanation and lead to the demand for a magical solution. Most often, this woman explained these as invasions of the devil into her being. However, one wonders how much effect the biochemical therapies would have on these tactual responses in removing the need for magical explanations and magical solutions. The pastoral counselor would then be in a position to discuss the person's relation to God and Christ without the impediment of at least this portion of the superstitious frame of mind of the patient. Here pastoral counseling and medical treatment have their nexus.

Another observation is how the patient moved toward the minister and his wife, was apparently appreciative of their prayers, but then began to associate them and their giving her their card with the devil who "left his calling card." The pastoral counselor may as well be prepared to become a part of the evil side of the patient's delusions. He may well be cast into the role of the persecutor or the tempter or even, as in this case, the devil. Staying on the brighter, more benevolent, and friendly side of the patient's delusional structure is difficult indeed, and often impossible. The couple to whom she talked seemed to have been overwhelmed by the patient's strangeness. They may not have had the advantage of the knowledge of the patient's whole religious outlook that her autobiographical account gives the reader here. If they had, they could have built upon the healthier ideas that she presented, such as her struggle to rely upon the grace and love of God without so much personal effort on her part. The act of giving the patient their calling card was interpreted literally by her and apparently served to break the relationship. The Lord Jesus is interpreted by her as not wanting her back there anymore.

The task of a spiritual director in this person's life would be to establish and maintain a durable relationship to her—in short, to stay by her through thick and thin. Yet the very nature of the illness itself caused her to break relationships. Once established, such a relationship would be the touchstone of reality that she needed. This points to the need for a pastoral strategy based on a good theory and developed into a wise practice for dealing with magic and superstition in religious experience.

THEORIES OF MAGIC, SUPERSTITION, AND RELIGIOUS HEALING

Several theories as to the interaction of magic, superstition, and religious healing have been advanced by research persons in the area of culture and personality.

Personal Response to Acculturative Stress

David Omar Born has proposed that these sick forms of religion are caused by the individual's effort to respond and grow under the stress caused by the conflict between an older, more established culture into which one is born and in which his habits are formed and a newer, less established culture into which he is moving, by reason of education, generation gap, and technological adjustments being made. He says that in the face of the stress created, a person may go in one of four directions: First, retreatism, a return to or the conscious preservation of traditional patterns, and resistance to new patterns. Second, reconciliation, or attempting to "strike a happy medium" of combining both the traditional and the new. Third, innovation, or the complete acceptance of the new patterns and the conscious rejection of the traditional. Fourth, withdrawal, an overt rejection of both the traditional and the new. This denial of both is the mechanism of defense.

In all but the first mode of adjustment, the possibilities of the person's becoming sick are present because he takes the risks of change. He can easily become a "marginal" man caught between things old and things new. His religion, when seen as a conserving, maintaining, and continuity-giving force in his life, becomes a symbol of his heritage, with which he must stay in touch. On the other hand, if his religion is at the same time prophetic and bids him have done with the bondage of the past, it may introduce a conflict of "fever-level" proportions that results in his illness as a person. (David Omar Born, "Psychological Adaptation and Development Under Acculturative Stress," unpublished paper, Southern Illinois University Department of Anthropology.)

The symbolic beliefs that a person brings over from his original culture continue to exert emotional "unreason" over his life despite the intellectual overlay brought by education, technological cause-and-effect training, and the like. The patterns of thought and behavior ingrained as fears into the patients described above tended to operate habitually in spite of attempts to "reason" with the patient. These patterns themselves can be disengaged, isolated, tranquilized, or dissociated in such a way that the persons can work, eat, sleep, and carry on the daily rounds of their lives, but some specific reeducation of the patterns of behavior themselves must take place if they are to be identified as being from the realm of magic and superstition. The findings of the behavioral therapists can be first fully focused upon these phobic personalities' needs.

Superstition and Magic as a Conditioned Response

B. F. Skinner has set forth the theory that superstition is the accidental connection of a given reinforcing stimulus with a given response: "If there is only an accidental connection between the response and the appearance of a reinforcer, the behavior is called 'superstitious.' " (B. F. Skinner, *Science and Human Behavior,* p. 85; The Macmillan Company, 1953.) This raises the issue of what kind of rewards and punishments go with the belief of such religious persons as have been described in this chapter. We know that one of the patients was rewarded with approval for holding faithful to the beliefs. She was punished with the belief if she disobeyed her grandmother. In adult life, holding the beliefs gave her membership in a church group, and rebelling against them denied her fellowship and left her isolated.

Persuasion, Illness, and Healing

A related but distinctly different concept of the power of superstition and magic is that of *forced indoctrination,* more popularly known as "brainwashing." William Sargant has done the most thorough work on forced indoctrination. He comments that the theological improbability of eternal punishment is less frightening to people today than to those of Charles Finney's day. Yet the threat of hard labor for life in a Communist prison camp can produce results similar to those of Finney in their power to change the mind. (William Sargant, *The Battle for the Mind,* p. 141; Penguin Books, 1957.) It may be added that the fear of mental illness itself is an even more subtly powerful threat in the culture of America today.

Jerome Frank has identified the element of persuasion and thought reform in modern psychotherapy as an essential part of the ability of the psychiatrist. He says, "Although the psychotherapist may state his interpretations in neutral terms, many are nevertheless covert exhortations or criticisms based on implicit value judgments." (Jerome D. Frank, in Ari Kiev, ed., *Magic, Faith, and Healing,* p. xii; The Free Press of Glencoe, 1964.) The religious healer, likewise, must have an ideology that offers the patient "a rationale, however absurd, for making sense of his illness and the treatment procedure." (Jerome D. Frank, *Persuasion and Healing,* p. 60; The Johns Hopkins Press, 1961.)

On the one hand, then, the empirically-minded student

of sick religion is faced with the reality of persuasive and even magical formulas in the belief-value system of the religiously sick person. On the other hand, he comes up against the rather elaborate value systems and ideologies of the psychotherapists. When the student understands both systems well, he knows that they overlap considerably. If he is a scientifically trained and religiously devout minister or psychiatrist, he must exist *with integrity* in both the empirical-pragmatic world of causal relations and the persuasive-ideological world of convincing values. How can this be?

The Existential Shift

Jan Ehrenwald says that, in the last analysis, these two conflicting worlds "derive their rationale from two contrasting sets of myths." He describes them both as having long histories, not one as "old and magical" and the other as "new and scientific." They both waver against each other as a magical vs. a pragmatic view of causality, as a sacred vs. a profane view of life, as prayer opposed to personal efforts, as the noumenal vs. the phenomenal. Ehrenwald says that the effective therapist is measured by his capacity to shift from one of these existential modalities to the other. He calls this "the existential shift" and gives the following definition of this "shift." He says:

> The therapist's abrupt transformation into a hypnotist is a graphic illustration of the principle. His dramatic shift from a pragmatic to a magic level of function is predicated upon a self-imposed regression—in this case in the service of treatment. . . .
> The scientifically trained psychiatrist is donning

the mantle of the magician and playing the part of the omnipotent hypnotist. It may well be that he himself is satisfied that all that is involved in such a venture is to assume a new, or rather an old-fashioned and traditionally well-defined professional role. Yet, in my experience, such role play is not enough in order to be effective. The hypnotist must not just pretend to be playing the role of the hypnotist. He must project himself, heart and soul, into the act. (Jan Ehrenwald, *Psychotherapy: Myth and Method, An Integrative Approach,* pp. 145–146; Grune & Stratton, Inc., 1966.)

Yet, the clinical application of this existential shift is unresearched insofar as I can learn. Ari Kiev found a near equivalent in the Mexican-American *curanderos* of San Antonio. The *curandero* is neither a doctor nor a priest. He is not a shaman in that he does not become possessed, exorcise, or prophesy; nor are special initiations, dream experiences, or ordeals used to qualify him to help people in distress. He is a personally religious person, functioning within the belief system of the Roman Catholic Church and "his religious demeanor, untrammeled by the authority of the Church, is his paramount virtue." (Ari Kiev, *Curanderismo: Mexican American Folk Psychiatry,* pp. 30–31; The Free Press of Glencoe, 1967.) The *curandero* draws upon both the beliefs of the Catholic faith and the folk medicine empirically learned through trial and error and handed down apprentice-style from one generation to the next. He does not look askance at but even recommends medical and/or psychiatric attention if the resources of expense and willingness on the part of the patient will bear it.

Kiev concludes that many of the elements present in psychotherapy are evident in the work of the *curandero*. His work is preventive of some psychiatric disorders, ameliorative in others, and supportive though not remedial in others. "Curanderism," says Kiev, "is also important not only as a form of prevention which contributes to lower incidence, but as a form of treatment agency whose presence leads to a reduced flow of people going to hospitals." (*Ibid.*, p. 192.)

PASTORAL APPROACHES TO SUPERSTITION

Magic vs. Sick Religion

The problem involved in the folk psychiatry of the *curandero* for both the educated minister and the psychiatrist is that neither of them can, as Ehrenwald has suggested must be the case, "project himself heart and soul into the act" of using nonrational, hypnotic, and/or magical practices. Both are committed to rational interpretations of both theology and human behavior. Both are committed to a "commonsense" approach to faith and health. Both fear quackery to such an extent that they feel more comfortable withdrawing from a patient such as the "victim of seducing spirits" than to "be party to the superstition" or implementer of magical formulas. This leaves the patient with a "calling card" but no help. The rituals of both organized religion and modern clinical psychiatry suffer from a lack of concept and procedure for coping creatively with the habits of thought of patients such as those who have been described here. Yet, implicit in both sets of ritual are tools useful to a patient as defenses against recovery. The patient usually uses one set of compulsive ideas to ward off the psychiatrist and another to fend off the minister. Consequently, the illness has an economy of its own that gratifies needs and becomes a substitute for realistic living in the world as it is. Some clues from the transactional therapists and the behavioral therapists may be helpful in suggesting a new departure, at least, in dealing with these patients.

Eric Berne, in his transactional analysis, suggests that psychiatry itself can become a distance-making, change-resisting "game." The patient continues for months to recite symptoms, dreams, fears, and obsessive religious ideas. In a demanding mood, the patient then seeks "answers" as to *why* he or she is this way and how the problems can be fixed. In short, magic answers and solutions are required of the therapist. As Berne says, the patient feels that "if she can only find out who had the button, so to speak, everything will suddenly be all right." (Eric Berne, *Games People Play,* p. 156; Grove Press, Inc., 1964.) In Berne's system, a game is a transaction that involves deception, maintains the status quo, and keeps others at a distance.

The "child" dimension of the patient is one of defiance: "You will never cure me . . ."; it is also one of substitute gratification: "but you will teach me to be a better neurotic (play a better game of 'Psychiatry')." All the while, the adult-to-adult transaction is: "I am coming to be cured." (*Ibid.,* p. 155.) In the face of such confusion, the psychiatrist and/or pastoral counselor find the game doubly employed, in that religion is used against the psychiatrist to maintain the game and psychiatry is used against the pastoral counselor.

One effective deterrent to this complicated situation, I have found, is to have both psychiatrist and pastoral counselor sit down together in the same therapy session—after taking a careful history of attempts at therapy—interpret this game to the patient and hopefully enter a contract that the game will be called off and specific difficulties in living faced as they are, without too much attention being given to the phobias, religious superstitions, and magical formulas.

This calls for an implosion—a breaking through the symptom wall—into the underlying problem areas of work, marriage, goals in living, and ways of deceiving other people at a quite conscious level. Wolpe, one of the formulators of what is coming to be called "implosive therapy," sees this as indicated for neurotic behaviors that are associated with intense anxiety but not appropriate for psychotic patients. (Joseph Wolpe, "The Systematic Treatment of Neurosis," *Journal of Nervous and Mental Disorders,* Vol. 132, 1961, pp. 189–203.) The patients described above are in this category, except for episodes of depression that came at specific crises and times of gross stress. Yet the compulsive-obsessional character of the thought processes persisted after the depression lifted. The differential diagnostic skill required here imperatively indicates the need for medical supervision. Yet the magical-superstitious religion that gives content to the anxiety states cannot be coped with effectively without the presence of a trained minister who can break through the wall of religiosity with more cooperation from the patient than can the psychiatrist.

In the cases dealt with in this manner by the author and a clinical psychiatrist conjointly, the process of treatment

moved forward more rapidly and certainly because the
stalemate between the religious and the health defenses
of the patient was broken from the outset. Running from
religious rationalizations to psychological ones was futile
because each could be challenged by the minister or
psychiatrist as the instance required.

The behavioral therapist's use of rewards or denials in
reconditioning "odd behaviors" in obsessive patients has
produced some possible areas of cooperation between
behavioral therapists and ministers. The Catholic system
of penance has utilized negative conditioning, and an
expansion of this system to include "here-and-now" positive reinforcement is an unexplored area of possible cooperation with behavioral therapists. O. H. Mowrer's
point of view seems to be that the unrealistic guilt of such
patients should be refocused on things they really ought
to feel guilty about and then dealt with realistically. (For
a thorough, detailed analysis of behavioral therapy, read
Halmuth H. Schaeffer and Patrick L. Martin, *Behavioral
Therapy;* McGraw-Hill Book Company, Inc., 1969.)

The crucial issue in all the above suggestions, however,
is that of interdisciplinary collaboration between ministers, psychiatrists, and clinical psychologists. The training
of each must be thorough enough that cooperative work
with patients is more than being superficially courteous to
each other. The therapeutic imperialism of any one of the
three must be forfeited. The proud insecurities of each,
resulting in promising much and delivering little in therapeutic results, must be faced and admitted.

Apart from this kind of candid collaboration, patients
have turned and will continue to turn to mass-produced
cultural forms of treatment. Christian Science is one of

these forms and appeals directly to the need of persons for positive reassurance, fixed rituals, and a loose-knit group fellowship. The perennial appeal of the affirmations of Norman Vincent Peale is another mass approach to the repetitive need for almost if not wholly magical uses of religion. The repetitive "aisle walker" in evangelistic crusades is another example of the way large numbers of people born and reared in the revival tradition turn to the ritual of the confession of faith or rededication of life again and again in their repeated anxiety states. Catholic priests write of the "scrupulous" person who returns repeatedly to confession for forgiveness for the same set of feelings.

The psychiatrist, the pastoral counselor, and the clinical psychologist are in much the same position in practice as are the above-mentioned groups. The expectations of magic brought by the suffering person are the same. The repetitive cycle in the treatment—with the exception of medical intervention in the case of periodic depressions and suicidal possibilities—is about the same.

One more positive way of looking at the compulsive, chronically fear-ridden persons discussed in this chapter is to see them as having been *maimed* by their superstitious upbringing. This has left them in a state of emotional deprivation and dependency that may well be life-long. Reconditioning of their behavior will produce obedience to a new source of dependency in order to compensate for their deep deprivation of approval and acceptance. However, the dependency and deprivation remain; the changed element is that the source of dependence rests in the therapist and the approval for changed behavior comes from the therapist. Periodic attention throughout the life-span of this person is provided by the therapist in many instances. "Therapy" becomes a way of life.

Theologically, the issue at stake is one of the *sources* of ultimate justification and trustworthiness in the world. Martin Luther's autobiography depicts this as his struggle —between the unmerciful demands of an unrelenting conscience and the need for redemption by faith alone. Yet the rituals of forgiveness themselves become a burden of repetition for patients such as we have described in this chapter. Possibly the words of one of the patients quoted above hold a key to this dilemma also. In speaking to a group of chaplains she said, "Show us that you care about us and maybe we can decide for ourselves that God cares."

IN SUMMARY

This chapter has sought to identify the magical and superstitious as a pathological distortion of healthy religious faith. The religion of superstition is at heart a system of manipulation, which seeks to rule out the necessity of faith in the face of the risks of the unknown and uncontrollable. Both magical rituals and obsessive-compulsive neurotic acts are in essence incantations of fear. Specific case history materials show how these magical practices of the emotionally disturbed person are "warding-off" devices and do not yield either to religious reasoning or to psychiatric treatment. The promise of behavioral therapy as a choice of treatment is discussed. The need for combined teamwork of minister and psychiatrist interviewing the patient together and at the same time was explored.

Chapter 4

THE MAJOR TRANSITIONS
OF LIFE
AND SICK RELIGION

THE PRIMITIVE RELIGIONS as well as the long-standing
sacramental systems of organized religions in a technological society have been built around the major transitions of life from birth to death. Paul Radin points out
that the building of rituals of social and religious inspira-
tion around these transitions of life is one of the reasons
religion has "gained a hold upon man's workaday life
and imagination." (Paul Radin, *Primitive Religion*, p. 79;
The Viking Press, 1937.) At birth, puberty, marriage, old
age, and death, these rites of separation, transition, and
reunion help define and redefine the community's relationship to an individual and the individual's changing
place in the community. They represent a social as well as
religious drama "ceremonially conceived of as a progres-
sive separation from one type of life and an entry into
another." (*Ibid.*, p. 92.) For example, puberty rites are
ways of separating a person from childhood and bringing
him into a place of more self-sufficiency. As the much-used
phrase puts it, they "separate the men from the boys."
When an individual is supported and guided through
these transitions by a healthy and hope-giving com-

munity, both he and the community are kept sound. Without it, both are sick.

Roy Grinker and his associates give the negative picture. They point out that a high degree of statistical significance is weighted against the families of borderline mentally ill persons because these families never "set eventual separation of parent and child as a goal." To the contrary, the "self-identity of children has been submerged by the family." (Roy Grinker, Beatrice Werble, and Robert C. Drye, *The Borderline Syndrome,* p. 122; Basic Books, Inc., 1968.) The overall objective of healthy religion would be to facilitate this "leaving of father, mother, brother, sister, etc." Rites of transition such as the Jewish *Bar Mitzvah* are calculated to do this meaningfully. The hypothesis of this chapter is that the individual does not get religiously sick in isolation. When the spiritual nourishment of participation with the religious community in the major crisis situations of his life is absent, never has existed, or is temporarily cut off in the life of an individual, the community itself as well as the individual suffers a failure of function religiously. The individual may be a person whose religion is anemic and sickly, but he lives in the midst of a people whose religion likewise is anemic and sickly. The effective religion, to the contrary, is the one, according to Freud, that "lowers the importance of the earthly family," and gives the individual a "safe mooring" place for his instinctual strivings, and at the same time gives him access to the "larger family of mankind." (Sigmund Freud, *Collected Papers,* Vol. III 2d ed., p. 597; London: Hogarth Press, 1943.) Thus the individual grows from one stage of life to another without becoming isolated, estranged, and alienated.

The function of religion at its best is to provide a believable patterning of life from stage to stage from birth to death for the individual and the family in the context of the larger family of mankind. This "larger family of mankind" is all people other than one's kinship group. (Arnold van Gennep, *Rites of Passage,* tr. by Monika B. Vizedom and Gabrielle L. Caffee; The University of Chicago Press, 1960.) The presence of these times of cognition, recognition, and renewal are generative sources of new hope and purpose in the life of the individual. Without these—either at the purely sociological level or at the religiosocial level, the individual becomes isolated. Isolation becomes the core of sickness. As the individual is related to but not a genuine part of a religious fellowship, to that extent he is religiously sick.

This point of view has been stated as a principle of preventive mental hygiene in strictly sociocultural terms by Gerald Caplan. He says that "a man does not usually face a crisis alone, but is helped or hindered by the people around him, by his family, his friends, neighborhood, community and even nation. These . . . provide him with the knowledge and confidence to solve problems in certain acceptable ways." (Gerald Caplan, *Principles of Preventive Psychiatry,* p. 43; Basic Books, Inc., 1964.) He speaks of serious and unavoidable problems that arise, creating "transitional points" in patients' histories, actually upsetting them psychologically, but lasting only from about one to four or five weeks. The problems are realistic ones such as bereavement, job loss or change, accidents, surgical operations, and basic changes of role in life due to developmental transitions, such as going to college, getting married, or becoming a parent. Caplan's point of

view is that adequate physical, psychosocial, and sociocultural support and supply at these times of transition—
in neither too much nor too little quantity—restore and/
or help maintain the equilibrium of a person, both relieving and preventing mental disorder.

These times of transition may be of two kinds—
emergency transitions and developmental transitions.
Emergency crisis situations such as illness, death, divorce,
etc., tend to have community supports and rituals in
abundance as contrasted with the developmental crises,
such as the last child's starting to public school, the last
child's becoming an adult and "moving out on his own,"
or the involutional period and retirement. These developmental transitions or crises—the two words being used
here to mean something of the same thing—are subtle
moments in the lives of persons. They tend to go un-
noticed by the community as a whole. The dramatization
of their importance does not appear except in the case of
a wedding. Even here, in the contemporary wedding the
parents are in a *demand* situation with a minimum of
reward and acknowledgement or *support* coming from
the community.

Robert Havighurst has called these times of transition
"teachable moments," when the person is opened not
only to the expectations of those around him but also to
the social and cultural instruction the community has to
afford him. If we view the religious community as a teaching and worshiping community, then these "teachable
moments," captured and treated as sacred occasions of
instruction and worship, can contribute to the stability
and continuity of the person. Left ignored, unattended,
and unsupported at these moments, the individual and

family has to feed on itself in isolation. Secular agencies, such as the public school, fill in the gap in many instances. When a person does not "make it" through one of these transitions, and if illness actually occurs, the hospital itself has to "treat" the results of the inadequacies of the family, the church, the school, and other secondary institutions to enable persons to make the hurdle of these transitions. (Robert Havighurst, *Human Development and Education,* pp. 2–4; Longmans, Green & Co., Inc., 1953.)

Paul Tournier has given a distinctly religious interpretation of these times of transition in his book *L'Homme et son lieu,* which has been translated into English under the title *A Place for You* (Harper & Row, Publishers, Inc., 1969). He says that man is always leaving one station or place in life and seeking another not yet realized. He says it is an act of faith to make the leap from one to the other, yet the space and time in between are times of anxiety and stress. One needs the encouragement and support of a community of faith in order to "make the leap." (Paul Tournier, *L'Homme et son lieu,* p. 159; Neuchâtel, Switzerland: Delachaux & Niestlé, 1966.) Tournier uses the parable of a trapeze artist to make his point. One swings forth on one bar to the extremity of its length and leaps to the oncoming bar. In between is a breathtaking moment of suspense, weighted with the possibility of "missing" the next bar. To hazard this anxious suspense is an act of faith. Although Tournier does not say so, one could say with Havighurst that each leap one takes, or each developmental task one accomplishes, gives an individual skill and confidence in taking the next leap, in accomplishing the next developmental task. Thus faith and skill are related to each other in practice and in the confidence a person has with which to face the demands of a new place, situation, or station in life. The following instance of a twenty-one-year-old Vietnam veteran is a case for study of the way in which illness takes over in the life of a person at the point of these transitions in life.

A twenty-one-year-old veteran returned to his lower-middle-class home. His father, aged fifty-one, worked as a salesperson in a men's clothing store. His mother was a housewife only. There was a ten-year-old sister. The family had little or no plan for the returned veteran's life and neither did he. He was advised by the Veterans Administration of his GI benefits and came under considerable stress to make up his mind as to what he was going to do.

Just as he was in the middle of his own decision-making, his father died suddenly of a heart attack. The mother saw that the whole burden of caring for herself and her ten-year-old daughter would fall upon her. She decided that she would go to college and finish her degree so that she could teach. In order to do this, she insisted that the son, twenty-one, get a job as a clerk in an office of a railroad company. This he did. He worked for about three months before he became mentally ill.

The situation came to my attention because of the young GI's church connections. He had been born and reared as a member of a devout Church of God family in a lower-middle-class neighborhood. Through friendships he formed at work, he met a girl who was home from college and working for the summer. She came from an upper-middle-class family, the daughter of a university professor. She went to a sedate, well-to-do church that had a wealthy and somewhat sophisticated membership. The young man left his church and started to church where the girl was.

He became passionately in love with the girl in a very short time. He wanted to see her every spare minute she and he were off from work. She was panicked and overwhelmed by his attentions. The mother of the patient reported that when he could not see the girl, he was restlessly pacing his room, would not eat, and slept very little.

On one evening, he went to the girl's house without a prior arrangement, a date. She was involved in a bridge game with some girl friends. He became very insistent, demanding, and loud in courting her to go out with him. She at first was primly "nice" to him, then irritated, and finally very hostile. She called him "crude and common," whereupon he slapped her. At this point, her father intervened and tried to get him to leave, but he would not. At this the father called the police and had him arrested.

The whole matter became a part of the "gossip" of the youth group that both the young man and his girl friend attended on Sunday evenings. The assistant pastor in charge of the group visited the boy at the jail. He perceived that he was in deep trouble and collaborated with me as a fellow minister. At about the same time the patient was released from jail on bond, an appointment with me was arranged.

The young man's primary concerns on the first interview were his anxiety over how to "get back in the good graces" of his girl friend and how to get his job back. His company had a rule that anyone who was arrested automatically lost his job. The man wanted to be taught some "psychological tricks" to use to get his girl friend back. This was the point to which he returned at every attempt on my part to expand the range of the conversation. The interview ended on this theme with a definite plan for a second interview.

Between the first and second interviews I received a call from the mother of the young man saying that he was

"stalking" the girl when she got off from work. When he
would return home he would go to his room and stay
there without coming out for meals or anything. The
mother said she felt that he needed psychiatric help. She
knew a psychiatrist who had been her family doctor
before he went into the specialty of psychiatry.

I urged her to get the son to this doctor and I pledged
my assistance if the young man came the next day for his
appointment.

On the next day, the young man did return and I
listened as he told of his mother's suggestion that he seek
psychiatric help. He asked what I thought and was urged
to go to the psychiatrist. He did so that afternoon and the
doctor hospitalized him immediately. The main treatment was hospitalization and psychotherapy, augmented
by drug therapy for sleep inducement. The young man
spent two weeks in the hospital, saw the psychiatrist for
interviews daily, and followed the group activities of
patients in the meantime.

The mother was seen by a social worker who, in turn,
contacted me about a new life-situation plan for the
patient, the mother, and the ten-year-old sibling. It was
agreed that instead of the mother's going to college, the
son would take advantage of his GI benefits to go to
college himself. Fortunately, his high school record quali-
fied him for scholarship aid. The mother took a part-time
job and so did the young man himself. After he got
established in school, she was able to take some part-time
schooling.

From a religious point of view, the young man returned
to his original church and began to form a few friendships there as well as to reactivate some friendships that
had lapsed during his two years in the service. His home
religious community became actively interested in him
and his well-being only after his hospitalization.

This case shows the residue of *several* major crises that accumulated in this man's life. He was inducted into service shortly after he finished high school. He did not have the freedom to work for a while to gain his independence and to learn a job skill. He was in Vietnam during the heaviest fighting and yet came through unscathed and without apparent psychological symptoms. Upon his return he was faced with the death of his father and pushed into the role of a main breadwinner immediately. Someone conducted the funeral of the father, but no follow-up grief counseling for the family was provided. Here is the major transition point in the young man's life where his religious community did not function to provide concern and basic wisdom as the young man and his mother remade their life plans. Earlier than this, there was no transitional support and emotional supply from his church at the time of his return from Vietnam. As a result, he came to the loss of his father without the religious and sociocultural supplies with which to meet the vast transition required of him. He was isolated; the church represents communion. He was alone; the church represents fellowship. He reached out to the other church through the interest he had in the girl. But a new man, just recently back from an unpopular war, and from a less affluent part of town, was not really a part of what was happening. He was a stranger.

Yet the established relationship of the mother to a family-doctor-turned-psychiatrist held firmly. He became the organizing center of a temporary community of professional persons—the hospital. This community created an atmosphere of security and wisdom around the young man. They mobilized the resources of the church, the

local university, and the home to build a bridge across
the very difficult time in the life of this whole family of
whom the patient was a part but not the whole.

LATE AND DELAYED ADOLESCENCE
AND A PSYCHOLOGICAL MORATORIUM

More psychologically, the young man was undergoing
the kinds of reappraisal of his life that are very typical of
the problems that late and delayed adolescents are facing
in large numbers today. Spafford Ackerly, M.D., calls
attention to the need for a "time of fallowing" in the life
of a young person before the permanent commitments of
life are made. This is especially needed in the lives of
middle-class adolescents, because their homes tend to be
affluent enough to extend the dependence of their youth
well beyond the midpoint of even the twenties. (Spafford
Ackerly, "Late Adolescence: A Lying Fallow Period of
Consolidation," in Walter van Boyor and Richard Grif-
fith, eds., *Conditio Humane,* p. 7; Berlin: Springer Ver-
lag, 1966.) Erik Erikson calls this era a "psychological
moratorium" of wandering and wishing and dreaming
before premature closure on the basic patterns of identity.
(Quoted in Helen L. Witmer and Ruth Kotinsky, eds.,
New Perspectives for Research on Juvenile Delinquency,
p. 3; U.S. Government Printing Office, 1955.)

The young man in the previous case history was thresh-
ing about and trying to "find himself," but in the society
in which he found himself he experienced no adults who
understood this need. He was a veteran. Many who do not
go to war or even become a part of the military at all have
even more difficult times in the patterns of evasion, resistance, escape, and survival they are forced into because of

the military draft. If the draft were not in existence, or even if it were universally required of everyone as it is in Israel, the military itself could provide the necessary rites of passage—separation, transition, and reentry—for the time of psychological fallowing and moratorium. However, the *use* of the military as a constructive force in the life of the individual is subordinated to the political and military objectives of the Federal Government. The tragedy of this is the possibility that such a making of the military for man rather than man for the military would probably make a better military in the long run. In the absence of this, the alienation of whole generations of youth who, nevertheless, take their moratorium in drugs, illness, radical political activity, and violent demonstrations is the whirlwind we reap for having sown to the wind.

The church has natural groups available in which delayed adolescents like the above patient become involved for a variety of reasons. His relationship to his peer group was never really solved. The group life of both his home church and the church he visited did not really break through his wall of isolation. The latter group did, through the assistant pastor as leader, put into motion the process whereby professional help was found for him. The assistant pastor came to the scene very late with what this tragic drama had been asking for since the young man returned from Vietnam, and especially since the death of his father. The assistant pastor was a good fireman to put out a fire that was ablaze when he reached it. The pastor who conducted his father's funeral is really the "man who was not there" when the family needed him most.

Complaint may be raised: "Well, how could the pastor

have known about these things when no one asked for his help?" The answer seems to be that a routine follow-up of a funeral situation needs to be a standard operating procedure a pastor should regularly perform. At that time, after the crowd has disappeared, the pastor can inquire into the well-being of the family in an appropriate manner. We know that this was not done in the above instance. Neither was any initiative exerted or ritual apparent to welcome the man home from war. There was no real "place" for this man as he swung back into his home community. The church and its pastor were no doubt busy, but not busy about this man's situation in life at the time the precipitating events were happening: his return from military to civilian life, the death of his father, his attempts at courtship, and his first job.

SOCIAL CLASS AND CULTURAL MARGINAL MEN

The religious factor of church relationship involves another factor in this young man's life: the social-class factor. Demerath and others have identified the "ways in which discrepancies in social class mobility show a relation to full blown illness," *and* to religious affiliation and devotion. (Nicholas J. Demerath, *Social Class in American Protestantism,* pp. 133 f.; Rand McNally & Company, 1965.) The case just cited has a definite social-class factor in it. The young man was caught between loyalties to two socially estranged churches. Boisen's findings in his book *Religion in Crisis and Custom* (Harper & Brothers, 1955) further demonstrate a causal relation between estrangement of socially diverse churches and the incidence of emotional disorder. Also, Morris Rosenberg studied a group of high school juniors and seniors in ten high schools in New York State. His concern was the relationship between dissonant or conflicting religious contexts and emotional disturbance. He concluded that the "effect of dissonant context does not appear to be large and powerful," but the results are perfectly consistent. For all nine comparisons made, those in dissonant religious contexts were without exception more likely than others to manifest symptoms of psychological disturbance: low self-esteem, psychosomatic symptoms, and depressive affect. (Morris Rosenberg, "The Dissonant Religious Context and Emotional Disturbance," *The American Journal of Sociology,* Vol. LXVIII, No. 1, July, 1962, pp. 1–10.) We can see from the above case that the factor of religious affiliation was not "large and powerful" in the situation of the patient, but, outside of the influence of his mother, the church was the *one* protection from isolation and an avenue toward help with the problems the patient had. In the great transition from late adolescence to maturity, from war to civilian life, etc., the young man was supported and sustained but he had to become acutely sick before his community became aware of his need.

THE TRANSITION OF MIDDLE LIFE

Another great transition of life is that of middle age. The sociological definition of middle age given by some experts on the family is that time from the departure of the last child from home to the time of retirement from a job. Permitting the children of a home to become self-determining adults means a "turning loose" of the control of the situation of the family. In Grinker's terms, it means the parent's actually separating himself from the child, not just having this as a future goal. This is *it!* The following case is an example of this transition and its vicissitudes in the life of a mental patient.

This is a fifty-eight-year-old Jewish man. He is a successful manufacturer in a family-owned business of which he is president. His wife is fifty-three years of age, a housewife and aide to him in the business. They have two sons, the elder of the two having already started his own business and established his own home. The younger of the sons, however, is a twenty-five-year-old single man who has been a cerebral palsy victim from birth. He can function well intellectually and was able to finish college. Physically, however, he can function only from a wheelchair.

For years the disabled son was his father's helper in the business. He learned the business well and became quite aggressive in telling his father how to modernize and improve the business. The father, however, could not believe that this son, as crippled as he was, could take full responsibility for the business. Yet he felt himself needing help in running the business if he was to continue it. As he began to grapple with this decision, he became agitated and depressed. He was admitted to a hospital with these symptoms.

The therapy consisted of electroconvulsive therapy and chemotherapy. The social workers ferreted out the problem of the family-business decision he was facing and reported to the doctor that they felt upon investigation that the son, although a disabled person, was thoroughly competent to handle the business. They also discovered that the father had a new, smaller business in mind for himself, one that would give him some new challenge as well as an income.

The psychiatrists instituted brief psychotherapy and these immediate decisions were discussed. The man decided to entrust the business to his son. The main reason he could decide this was that he had seen the son take over and run the business while he, the father, was in the hospital for about three months. He saw his son become more and more responsible.

The religious life of this Jewish man was noninstitutional. He observed none of the practices of Judaism and did not attend the synagogue. However, he was a "God fearer" and prayed regularly on a personal basis. There was no rabbi at the hospital, but the Protestant chaplain visited regularly at the patient's request. In these visits, the chaplain worked supportively during the acute phase of treatment. He collaborated with the psychiatrist and the social workers as the above discoveries were made. As the man made decisions on his own, the chaplain encouraged him to do so. The patient asked for prayer and the chaplain prayed for courage and a new sense of adventure for the patient. He gave thanks for the excellent care the patient and his wife had given their disabled son. He prayed for the firm establishment of the son in his daily work.

Whereas this patient found in the hospital experience itself a secular "rite of passage," he is typical of many middle-aged persons. *There were no rites of passage for the transition into middle age.* In the previous case of the college-aged GI, the act of going to college itself was a rite of separation, transition, and reunion into young adulthood. However, no such rites have been devised either within the churches and synagogues or in secular society. Little wonder is it that the isolation, lack of communal participation, and accumulated burdens serve to produce what is met at the physiological level with bodily change and result in involutional emotional disorders, of which anxiety neuroses and depressions are common.

The middle-aged patient also demonstrates the way in which the middle years are often a time when the person narrows down his range of relationships rather than widening the range to include new people and deepening it to enrich the relationships he already has. Middle age should be a time when new people are actively sought out for their friendship and when old friendships are culti-vated and given more time and attention. The patient just reported on did not do either of these things. This failure included his continued detachment from any par-ticipation in the life and rituals of the Jewish faith. I do not want to be understood as saying that if he had been a faithful communicant at his synagogue, he would not have become ill. Rather, I am saying that if his synagogue could have stayed in touch with him whether he was a regular attendant or not, he would have been enabled to make the transition of middle age with much less wear and tear.

THE PASTORAL MANAGEMENT OF DISORDERS AT THE TRANSITION OF LIFE

Pastoral Visitation

The visits of the Protestant chaplain were the one ritual of the religious community in which the patient mentioned above could participate. The request he made focused primarily at the very personal level of a pastoral visit, but this ritual was a commonly understood one by patient, chaplain, psychiatrist, nurse, and social worker.

It was a "bridging" relationship in many respects. There-fore, the pastor of a church—in the absence of elaborate corporate ceremonies—has at his service the pastoral call as a medium for support, interpretation, and relieving isolation in the great crises of life. Whereas he cannot restrict visitation to acute distresses of life such as mental disorders, he will need to do this less if he does not wait for acute distress to make pastoral calls. For example, the returned GI and the middle-aged man who is contem-plating selling his business can be served greatly by a perceptively planned pastoral call. If there is no distress, then celebration may be in order. If distress is in the making, then it can be detected sooner and thereby pre-vented or brought under earlier treatment. If the distress is at an acute stage, then the pastor is better late than never and may be a part of the earlier recovery of a person.

Group Exploration

The young GI attended a group. The Jewish man had none. Yet both of them are representatives of specific "need" groups in a community. One group is the "work-ing boys" and "working girls" in a community. These persons are not in the routine "going-to-college" group. They are neither high school nor college young persons. Their "ingroup" often does not exist. The pastor and his colleague can form a group of this category of young persons for the purposes of fellowship, exploration of common problem situations facing them, and for the early detection of isolation, unrealistic thinking and act-ing, and frustrated, unfulfilled dreams.

The Jewish man represents a perennial group of lonely and readjusting persons in every community—the middle-

aged, "empty-nest" people. There one finds the persons
who have let earlier religious resolutions lapse. They have
lost touch with a vital group of persons of their own age,
because they have often worked night and day accumulat-
ing money, goods, and success in their vocation. They
have overconcentrated on the success of their children.
They face crucial decisions about their relationship to
the grown sons and daughters, always fighting the ten-
dency to forget that these sons and daughters are no
longer children. They have to give up control of their
offspring and learn new tasks for their own future.

Pastors find these persons ripe for what today is called
"renewal"—within the church and without it. Usually the
renewal movement is built upon small-group interaction,
confrontation, and support. This is done on an occasional
basis at retreat centers such as Laity Lodge at Leakey,
Texas, Kirkridge Retreat at Stroudsburg, Pennsylvania,
and Yokefellow Institute at Richmond, Indiana. Problems such as those faced by the Jewish businessman in the
case cited above are typical of what is discussed in these
groups. Isolation is overcome, trust is encouraged, and
new friends are made. The personal religious values and
resources of the individual and group are assessed. Personal prayer is encouraged at both the individual and the
group levels. Care is taken not to attempt more than can
be dealt with in a relatively short time. People return to
these centers often and open up new areas of concern and
growth. Reports of these groups are found in the work
edited by John L. Casteel entitled *Personal Renewal
Through Small Groups* (Association Press, 1957). Removal
to a retreat center has the excellent advantage of breaking the normal routine for the individuals and of giving
them an opportunity for undivided attention.

One need not depend upon retreats away from the busy activity of the daily and weekly routine of church life. The creative use of fellowship groups, transitory groups set up at a time of stress for a given purpose, and the like can be set up in the regular week's life in a parish situation. For example, the mothers of children who have just started to school can well enjoy fellowship with each other in the fall months of that particular year. The parents of sons who are draft-aged can be cared for in groups. Couples nearing retirement can meet together on a small-group basis and collaborate about their plans for the future, arrange outings and activities together, etc. All this can be done without the necessity of a retreat from the routine of life, and in an informal way.

These groups provide a loose-knit set of rites of passage for people going through radical changes of life. Many times a person necessarily must reach outside his church for such care. However, some ministers who have seen the value of such groups in a renewal center have returned to their parishes and established renewal groups in the day-to-day life of the parish church. Entering, participating, and growing beyond such groups often amount to rites of separation, transition, and reentry for adults who have the common developmental tasks that middle age has yet to accomplish. Whereas the renewal movements extend to adults of all ages, the crisis of middle age tends to call for the kind of group behavior and personality change they offer in a special way. A thorough, recent symposium on this subject has been edited by John L. Casteel, entitled *The Creative Role of Interpersonal Groups in the Church Today* (Association Press, 1968).

A Durable Peer Group

If an adult has not developed a lasting relationship to persons his own age by the time he reaches full maturity in the middle years, isolation can be his lot. The pastor is in a unique position to encourage new friendships and the deepening of old friendships. He can do so through his own ministry by introducing individuals to each other and through the use of already existing groups in the church. However, these ministries are self-defeating if they remain at a superficial, social, "chit-chat" level. A level of trust must be achieved whereby the person is enabled to discuss the more serious issues of his personal life and know that he will be heard and taken seriously in return. The damp rot of both individual and corporate life is the increase of isolation. The perceptive pastor is at work detecting the presence of isolation and counteracting it with the life of the fellowship of believers.

In Summary

The major transitions of life as "teachable moments" for preventing emotional disorders are discussed in this chapter. The inadequacy and sickness of religion appears in the failure of the religious community to be present and to provide meaningful rites of passage—rites of separation, transition, and reentry for persons as individuals and families at times of transition. Pastoral visitation, group exploration, and the building of a durable peer group tend to overcome isolation, to provide shared interpretation, and to counteract the forces of pathology with the forces of health.

Chapter 5

SPIRITUAL TERRITORY
AND SICK RELIGION

MEN AND WOMEN move through the great transitions of
life, leaving one "place" in life and searching for another
territory—larger, more challenging, filled with more hope
for living. I use the word "territory" here in both a
literal and symbolic sense. Abraham, the prototype of
faith for both Judaism and Christianity, "went out, not
knowing where he was to go." He and others like him
were "called to go out into a place," which they "should
after receive for an inheritance." One asks what would
have happened to the "real Abram" if he had stayed in
Haran and if his father before him had stayed in Ur of
the Chaldeans. Would they have had dreams and visions
of a new territory of their own existing only in their
thoughts, which, if shared with other people, would have
seemed "crazy" to them?

In these pages, the pastor has been directed to the
relevance of behavioral therapy for his work as a counselor with the person who has been conditioned by superstitious upbringing resulting in phobic and compulsive
behavior. In relation to the pastoral approach to isolated
persons making the great transitions of life alone, the

pastor has been pointed to the relevance of group work, particularly sensitivity training, for assistance in the methods most pertinent to the needs of such persons. The concept of spiritual territory is a distinctly existential one. Therefore, we turn to the existential therapists for working concepts that are appropriate for understanding and relating to persons who are confused as to their territory in life.

The working hypothesis of this chapter is that the quest for one's own territory in life is basic to the nature of faith at its best. When this territory is unperceived, denied, overwhelmed, invaded, or taken from a person, he is likely to develop what is today commonly called an emotional disorder. Many times he will create an imaginary world or territory of his own. An array of prophetic writers have, in many different ways, pointed to this phenomenon of "personal room," "psychic space," etc.

Martin Buber speaks of the paradox of distance and relationship. He does not use the concept of territory, but defines the same idea in terms of "distance" and "otherness" from one's confreres. Before genuine dialogue and conversation can be realized, the unique "otherness" of the partners must be affirmed and accepted. Buber says that "every actual fulfillment of relations between men means acceptance of otherness. . . . The strictness and depth of human induration, the element of otherness of the other, is then not merely noted as a necessary starting point, but is affirmed from the one being to the other." (Martin Buber, *The Knowledge of Man*, ed. by Maurice Friedman, p. 69; Harper & Row, Publishers, Inc., 1965.)

Rollo May describes the personal territory of the individual as the *Eigenwelt*. The *Umwelt* is our biological environment. The *Mitwelt* is our interpersonal milieu. The *Eigenwelt* is that decisive self which stands apart from both as one's own private intellect, as Kant called it. This is, as May says, "the self in relation to itself." (Rollo May, *Existence*, pp. 64–65; Basic Books, Inc., 1958.) This existential model for personality will be challenged by behavioral therapists as a resurrection of the concept of the "soul." However, the behavioral therapist can appreciate the unused senses of touch and smell and their capacity for creating a private world of cognition that usually is untapped, even by the existentialists.

Before May gave this existential interpretation of the "inner territory," Karen Horney interpreted the inner conflicts of the neurotic personality of our times in terms of the movement of the spirit into or out from itself away from others, against others, down upon others, etc.

Even before these writers, Gilbert Murray described the religious impulse of man to be the need to discover and take "the uncharted regions" of human life. Alfred North Whitehead defined religion in terms of what we do with our solitude, that territory that is "the I" alone, uninvaded by others.

Two recent authors, however, have made detailed studies of "territoriality." Robert Ardrey hypothesizes that the world "is a world of order and ordained self-sacrifice to greater and longer goods; it is an ordered world in which territory exerts a prime moral force." (Robert Ardrey, *The Territorial Imperative*, p. 155; Atheneum Publishers, 1966.) He says, further, that the territorial imperative "commands beyond logic, opposes all reason, suborns all moralities, [and] strives for no goal more sublime than survival." (*Ibid.*, p. 236.) Ardrey has in mind the "home territory" of both man and lower animals. He speaks anthropologically and compares the instinctive homing of lower animals with the territorial imperative in human existence. A man, for example, will fight, he says, for his territory when he will not fight for his mate.

Edward T. Hall has called man's spatial sense of distance the "hidden dimension" of his behavior, perception, and values. He measures distance qualitatively and speaks of four qualities of distance: (1) Intimate distance, which involves actual body contact in the close phase and the six to eighteen inches of personal body boundary which can be invaded hostilely or can represent the comfortable closeness of mutual understanding at the nonverbal level. (2) Personal distance, representing a close phase and an "arm's length" phase. For example, a person's spouse may stand in this space with impunity but another person of the opposite sex may not. (3) Social distance, with a close phase of four to seven feet and a far phase of seven to nine feet. Here the turned head or turned back can give privacy and insulate people from each other. (4) Public distance, with a close phase of twelve to twenty-five feet and a far phase of twenty-five feet or more. This is the kind of distance the Secret Service likes to keep between public personages, such as the President of the United States, and a crowd.

Hall's hypothesis for his classification of distances is that "it is the nature of animals, including man, to exhibit behavior which calls for respect for territoriality. In doing so, they use the senses to distinguish between one space and another." (Edward T. Hall, *The Hidden*

Dimension, p. 120; Doubleday & Company, Inc., 1966.) He cites research that when the physical space of a given community dropped below eight to ten square meters per person, social and physical pathologies doubled. "Illness, crime and crowding were definitely linked." *(Ibid.,* p. 161.)

One of the most important aspects of the sense of space is that it calls into play the end organs of smell and touch. These sensory capabilities are so unused by man —not other animals—that we are likely to think of the data they collect for us as unimportant or even unconscious. Far from it, Hall would say, we as Americans are "culturally undeveloped" through the suppression of odors. He insists that smell, for example, "evokes much deeper memories than either vision or sound." *(Ibid.,* p. 43.) The galvanic responses of the skin and muscles are another almost automatic source of perceptual data. The kitchen of American homes, for example, is really designed for *one* person at work. The strain between two women in the same kitchen can be understood as their not liking to bump into each other, the galvanic resistance against being crowded, not that it is a feminine characteristic to want to be alone in the preparation of a meal.

The mentally ill person is particularly sensitive to territoriality, literally and figuratively speaking. The depressed person often wants to stay very close to someone he loves and who loves him. The schizophrenic person may panic when others get physically close to him or touch him. In describing their feelings, such patients refer to anything that happens within their "flight distance" as taking place literally *inside themselves.* These experiences recorded by therapists working with schizophrenics indicate that the realization of the self as we know it is intimately associated with the process of making boundaries explicit.

More figuratively speaking, one can say that the cultural and religious values one holds most sacred are *to him* his "staked-out" claim to uniqueness. These are often symbolized in terms of "places" where the person has lived. Hence the importance of place names in both the Old and New Testaments, and the ceremonies of renaming a place epitomize this importance. In emotional disturbances, for example, a student said that his problem was "the way between New York and Washington." Upon close inspection, the history of the student revealed that his mother and father were divorced when the student was nine. He stayed with his mother when his father left the home in New York. He remained with his mother until he was sixteen. At this time he and his mother had an intense argument over his choice of friends, staying out late at night, and not taking his schoolwork seriously. She told him that he was just like his father and that he no longer was welcome at her house and that he should go live with his father—in Washington. With heaviness of heart he left his friends, his school, and his mother, and went to live with his father. From then on he was torn from one loyalty to the other and the two sides of his conflict were symbolized in Washington and New York. He began to reconstruct his life creatively when he went to a third city—his own choice—and found work, education, and marriage in a new community of his own choosing. The new community reached out to incorporate him and to accept and affirm him as an adult person in his own right with a place, a wife, a work, and a faith that were uniquely his own. As he was accepted and as he established his own territory, along with the assistance of his minister and a psychiatrist in collaboration with each other, his symptoms of anxiety, confusion, and depression dissolved. He nevertheless had a nostalgia for his mother and had sought her in the faces of the girls with whom he tried to effect marriage. He reflected his homesickness for his father in that he chose his father's kind of work as his own. Yet the tasks of marriage and work at an adult level called for his "leaving mother and father" and going on to his own place in life. His accomplishment of these tasks could not be substituted for by therapy—either pastoral or psychiatric. As Karen Horney once said in a lecture, this was one situation in which life itself is the therapist, and life is the only therapist that does not ask whether the patient can take the treatment!

The Pathology of Religion and Spiritual Territory

One of the ways contemporary Americans create a psychic space of their own is through higher education. Here mobility is vertical and psychological instead of being horizontal and geographic. This has a positive aspect in the way a person from an uneducated family will strive hard for more and more academic degrees. It has a negative aspect in the way a person from a very educated family may break with the tradition and have nothing to do with school, college, or preparation for professional life.

In both instances, however, the acquisition of uniqueness comes at the price of isolation from one's heritage.
It makes marginal men and women of individuals. By
this, one means that a person is cut off from the family
into which one is born and that he is a stranger to the
social group into which he has moved by reason of his
educational and occupational status. The following
cases demonstrate both sides of this dilemma:

A thirteen-year-old Puerto Rican boy was admitted to
a psychiatric hospital in an acute psychotic state. He
was brought by his mother and older brother. He had been
in a psychiatric hospital previously, and, three months
after he was dismissed, his father died suddenly of a
heart attack. Thereupon, the boy's illness was reactivated.
His presenting symptoms were sleeplessness, auditory
hallucinations, hyperactivity showing in pacing the floor
vigorously; he was noncommunicative to the point of
being somewhat stuporous at times. *The background
history* revealed that this boy was the youngest son in a
family of first- and second-generation immigrants from
Puerto Rico. The now-deceased father had come to this
country during the Great Depression and by hard work
had earned a Ph.D. from Yale. He married into a well-to-
do family, to a woman who also was college-educated.
They, in turn, raised their children on the puritan
values of hard work, frugality, and learning. They broke
completely with the poor, uneducated parents and siblings of the father. All their children—four of them, of
whom the patient was the youngest—were college-educated. The patient, however, rejected his school oppor-
tunities, preferred to be alone, and lived in a world of
television characters. He liked to read but refused to follow the books required in school. The family was a very

religious family and one of the sons was studying for the ministry in a Christian church. His father had been a minister. However, the thirteen-year-old quickly rejected attempts to involve him in the religious activities of the hospital. He would have none of it.

The patient, however, was greatly concerned about magic and folklore that was reminiscent of the kinds of religious behavior his grandmother, the mother of his father, took for granted.

Yet all this reversion to his father's childhood religion was an irritation to his mother and brothers. As time went on he had become more and more intolerant of them and they of him. Isolation became a way of life and his schizophrenic illness represented his way of having a place, a territory of his own in the family constellations.

Prognosis on this patient is seen to be very guarded and largely contingent upon his being provided with a religious community that will take his "voodoo" seriously enough to talk with him about it, at least. The interracial factor is a large one in this case. The father died early— at fifty-three years of age—partly as a result of the great stress involved in his educational successes. The high-achieving brothers of the patient create a competitive atmosphere from which he would rather drop out than compete. His alternative is to enjoy his dreams and his *Eigenwelt* to the exclusion of the *Mitwelt* of his family. His illness represents a dogged defense of his own private territory of the within. Whether or not it becomes chronic with him hinges upon both his family's appreciation and their affirmation of his uniqueness as a basis for conversation with them. Also, it is contingent upon his developing enough capacity to trust them so that he can believe their good intentions when they converse with him. He has the advantage of youth, and time is on his side.

But the question I raise is as to the whereabouts of his paternal grandmother. She probably can converse with him and take him more seriously than can anyone else. Yet to this moment, she has not appeared, if indeed she is still living.

Furthermore, one can raise the question as to the role of group therapy for this young boy's future. The social-group worker has more rapport with him than most members of the staff, and the other young persons on the ward have avenues of communications with him. At best, his will be a long-term treatment. A minimal adjustment to the dreary reality of a mundane existence can be achieved, but will he not always be a stranger and a pilgrim seeking a place, a territory not yet apparent to the eye?

The reverse side of this picture must be clarified by case material also. The situation of a young woman describes this accurately:

This is a patient who was twenty-one years of age when I first met her. She has been known to me for eighteen years prior to the time of this writing. She came from an upper-lower-class home, her father being a machinist in a factory. Her mother and father were separated. Her church became a family substitute for her in the absence of her father and in the alienation she felt from her mother. She was encouraged to attend college by her pastor. Having finished college, she struggled with the decision as to whether or not she should enter religious work. She finally decided to do so and went to divinity school at a large university. She finished her degree with academic honors, all the while depending upon her church for financial support. Upon completion of her schooling, she worked as a director of religious education for two years and then resigned to take a position as a public relations director for a large company. She worked for the company for about five years. Her illness had its onset shortly after she was dismissed from this job. She never would discuss why she was dismissed.

The presenting symptoms were that she felt herself "splitting off into parts." As time went on she reported that she was three distinct persons at alternating times. One of these persons was "Cecile," a very fun-loving, amoral person. The other was "Deborah," a very precise, orderly person, moral to the nth degree. The other was a stranger, a shadowy person whose name she never knew.

The patient would awaken in a strange place from having been Cecile. She always "came to" as Deborah. She met the "stranger" in her nightmares. The one thing the three "selves" had in common was her automobile.

This patient became suicidal and was sophisticated enough to know, personally, several psychiatrists. She chose one and went to him for psychiatric help. She was hospitalized for almost a year, and was treated by psychotherapy and chemotherapy. The hospital itself became her "refuge," a place to which she as an estranged person could return. The hospital and her illness were the nearest things to any territory and personal individuality she could have.

After her hospitalization the patient started a doctoral program at a state university. She became upset at the demands of her advisers. After two years of work, she transferred to a private university. Again, she became upset with the faculty advisers and withdrew after a year and a half of work. As a result, she had spent nearly five years in an academic setting and had no degree to show for it. Employment was hard to get and her standards of expectation for a job were unusually high. The last report on this patient is that she is unemployed. She refuses to work in a professional role as a religious worker.

The dissociation of this patient's life seems to have begun when she lost her territory in the church and when she was forced by circumstance to operate as (a) a professional public relations person (b) a "swinger" of a party girl and (c) as the unidentified person whom she did not know. Her "multiple" personality, as Gardner Murphy, a research psychologist at Menninger Clinic, describes it, was really the same person functioning under different value systems at different times.

Yet, this person, even after the dissociation was overcome, was extremely reluctant to commit herself to any kind of realistic job opportunity, to any kind of durable relationship to a prospective husband, or to any kind of institution of higher learning. Her inability to accept the ambiguities of the graduate schools she attended was stalemated by her own feeling that she was unfitted for life if she did not have a Ph.D. degree. She seems to see the "land" of the Ph.D. degree as one that has been denied her. In the hierarchy of job placement, she cannot abide having people supervise her and at the same time shrinks from the responsibility of having the top supervisory role. She has a feeling of helplessness, which she explains as being caused by her not having a degree in her chosen field. In a real way, she has created a world of competence in which she abides alone, feeling all the while that she has had her realm taken from her and denied her. The chaos of this overwhelms her.

This situation has prevailed for about eight years now. It raises the question as to the kind of supervision given to graduate students. Seemingly, no real effort was made by one graduate school to learn from another graduate school as to what prompted the student to change schools. There was little or no follow-up to learn why she would change her vocation from the arena of church life to that of public relations for a private company.

PASTORAL APPROACHES

The Pastor: A Guardian of Solitude

The pastor who becomes aware of the depth of territorial imperatives in persons already has a sixth sense of how much initiative to take with persons and how little initiative it takes to crowd persons. He can differentiate between intimate distance, personal distance, social distance, and public distance. He has in these concepts new keys for evaluating what he himself means to people as persons. He develops a sense of appreciation for the psychic space an individual considers his own. He does not unwittingly invade another's territory, or psychic space.

Yet, at the same time, a pastor should be aware of the loneliness some people feel in the vast territory they have developed in a lifetime of effort. He cannot and dares not invade another person's territory. Neither can he afford to ignore an invitation to dialogue from the "other," as Buber calls him. The whole art of pastoral conversation hangs on this sensitivity of the pastor to nonverbal cues for conversation.

The Pastor: A Fellow in Fond Hopes

A specific pastoral approach to the private space—both intimate and personal—of another is that of "dreaming" with the person. This simply consists of asking the person what his fondest dream would be if it came true. The person will often feel a bit embarrassed, as if you have caught him only partially clothed. He or she might say that such dreams are too silly to discuss. With the promise that what they say will be taken seriously, such people will often begin opening up their *Eigenwelt,* their very own dreamworld, to the pastor.

Once this has happened, the pastor moves from a *Mitwelt* relationship to the role of alter ego dreaming along with the person. Much of the dream will be unrealistic, but some of it will be within reach of reality—far more than either the pastor or the "other" would dare ask. As Browning put it, "Ah, but a man's reach should exceed his grasp, Or what's a heaven for?"

The Pastor: An Evaluator of Sleep

The day-waking dreams of a person are live topics for discussion in pastoral conversation. The pastor, unless he is also a trained psychotherapist, does not ordinarily use dream analysis as a therapy of choice. However, the sleep routine of the person and the kinds of experience he or she has during sleep are important and should be taken seriously by the pastor.

After all, the withdrawal of a person into his or her own territory happens when sleep takes over. This *is* the *Eigenwelt* at its optimum condition. The feelings of pleasantness or unpleasantness of a dream are as important as its content. The meaning the dream has for the dreamer is more important than any that could be added by an "outsider." Also, the sleep routine of a person is a good barometer of the health of the person as a whole. The standard texts of psychiatry go into this in detail. Suffice it to say here that the pastor and the physician share a common concern for the ways in which both work and worship intertwine with the renewal that sleep brings, or does not bring. Both should evaluate the sleep routine, especially of sick persons.

The Pastor, Young Adults, and Sensitivity Training

Considerable attention has been given in the public press to the need for an expanded human awareness or sensitivity. Some of this has been in connection with the use of psychedelic drugs. The more recent concern has been focused upon natural rather than drug-induced ways of expanding human awareness and causing people to be more sensitive. William C. Schutz has written the definitive work on this in his book *Joy: Expanding Human Awareness* (Grove Press, Inc., 1967). He astutely observes the way in which the private space of an individual is protected, even at the level of the musculature of the body. Postures, such as a tension-racked head and neck stiffness accompanied by shallow breathing, are "often a manifestation of an unconscious resistance against being reached by another person. The individual is setting up a defensive wall to protect himself from whatever onslaught may ensue." (*Ibid.*, p. 36.) Sensitivity training trys to develop bodily, personal, and interpersonal discipline, the aim of which is to put a person's body in a right relation to its environment (the *Umwelt*), a person's emotions in a right relation to the interpersonal situation in which he lives (the *Mitwelt*), and an individual's personal functioning into right accord with his own private world (the *Eigenwelt*). Interestingly enough, a large part of the effort is to develop the unused sensory abilities of the person, especially the senses of touch, smell, and taste. (*Ibid.*, pp. 55 ff.) In one exercise, for example, a group is required to relate to each other in an unarranged room with their eyes closed for an hour without speaking. This raises the whole issue of one's perception of his own and others' territories in relation to one another.

Yet the experimentation with a group's sensitivity to one another poses the unresolved problems of individuals from their earliest years. The first one is that of *basic trust*. We permit only those whose intentions we basically trust to invade our territory in any way. The second one is normal for all young adults, the experience of *intimacy* that overcomes distance. (See Erik H. Erikson, *Identity and the Life Cycle;* Psychological Issues Monograph Series, The International Universities Press, 1959.) It involves calling off the scripts and games the group members half consciously play in order to maintain their territory in isolation from others and even in opposition to others. (See Berne, *Games People Play.*)

The pastor of a church may need to establish confrontation groups of this kind outside the walls of the church by calling on outside leadership. Yet, these are concerns which, half consciously, "sweat and fret" young adults. Some disciplined and positive leadership from the pastor can "head off" some larger problems that tend to appear in the unguided attempts of young adults to resolve the crisis of intimacy vs. distance. Many young executives are exposed to sensitivity training in business and industry. To them their pastor's interest will come as a pleasant surprise rather than a rude awakening. Thus, the compartmentalized territories of business and religion can at least have diplomatic relations even though their ideologies and goals, hopefully, differ!

The secularization of the body of the human being is a contradiction of the basic intentions of Hebrew, Christian, and other comprehensive faith systems. The construction of constricting "character armors" that crowd both the personal territory and social interaction of the individual has long denied him the joy of life, both personal and interpersonal. The minister reveres the privacy and psychic space of individuals. But, at the same time, he is aware of unnecessary loneliness occasioned by unnecessary distance from others. Paradoxically, the good minister functions in such a way that patiently and prayerfully he defends the other person's solitude and challenges the power of his loneliness.

The minister is a man of prayer. Ordinarily, the real prayers of people—secular or religious—are at the center of their private territory. As the minister opens the whole issue of his prayer response and relationship to individuals in small groups, he crosses that invisible boundary of the intimate territory of the person. Therefore, both the easiest and hardest way of entering this realm is by affirming one's own prayers in so many words and asking what kind of difficulty the "other" is having in prayer as well as what kinds of gratification prayer offers to the "other."

SPIRITUAL TERRITORY AND THE PASTOR AS COUNSELOR

In this chapter, as has been previously said, we have been turning to the existential therapists for working concepts that are appropriate for understanding and relating to persons who are confused as to their territory in life. Probably one of the more provocative and more easily read existential therapists is R. D. Laing, M.D., an English psychiatrist at the Tavistock Institute of Human Relations and Director of the Langham Clinic in London. He is a psychoanalyst as well as a psychiatrist. He has been particularly concerned with an existential approach to schizophrenia. He perceives the schizoid person as one who is torn in his relation to the world and who suffers "a disruption of his relation with himself." His outward and inward relationships are a territory divided and confused. Laing describes this ontological insecurity as being characterized by three forms of anxiety. All three of these forms of insecurity, it seems to me, symbolize the reactions of a person to a denial, an invasion, or the obliteration of his psychic space.

Laing says that the first type of anxiety is *engulfment*. He quotes one patient as saying to another with whom he was arguing: "I can't go on. You are arguing in order to have the pleasure of triumphing over me. At best, you win an argument. At worst, you lose an argument. *I am arguing in order to preserve my existence.*" This poignantly speaks to the situation of the pastor or teacher who "wins" in controversies with deeply disturbed parishioners. The pastor, being trained in the point-counterpoint of hairsplitting logic, can cleverly win an argument, and in the process *engulf* the very existence of a person who, at best, has only a beachhead hold on reality from the outset. The pastor wins the argument and loses the person. Laing says that such a patient, if subjected to the kind of questioning recommended in psychiatric textbooks, would evidence "signs of psychosis" in order to survive. (R. D. Laing, *The Divided Self: An Existential*

Study in Sanity and Madness, pp. 43–44; Penguin Books, Inc., 1960.) The struggle to maintain one's identity under pressure of engulfment is accomplished through isolation and withdrawal.

Laing's second descriptive word for the anxiety created by an invasion of the ontologically insecure person is *implosion.* The person fears his own emptiness and is clutched with terror that the world will "at any moment crash in and obliterate all identity . . ." Instead of *ex*-ploding, he is empty and fears *im*plosion. The world takes on a "persecuting, impinging aspect."

The pastor meets persons in and out of hospitals who feel gnawing emptiness, like Robert Frost's hired man, who had nothing to look back upon with pride nor to look forward to with hope. There is a shell-like fragility in conversations with them. As Laing says, "We are all only two or three degrees Fahrenheit from experiences of this order." (*Ibid.,* p. 46.)

The third type of anxiety of which Laing speaks is *petrifaction* and *depersonalization.* The person has tactile sensations that seem to him as if he is being turned to stone. He dreads the fate of being turned from a person into a thing. Treating the person as a thing, as an "it," reinforces this. From within, this amounts to a person's refusing to respond to or with his own feelings. It is a daily coping device known as being apathetic in order to survive. Laing presents cases that accentuate the situation of persons who never really had a territory of their own, a "place in life," a "being-for-oneself." He uses cases of persons who, he demonstrates, can be helped through the establishment of personal space and place in life through psychotherapy.

Laing does not think that classical psychoanalytic

approaches to the problems of such patients get to the core of the patients' feelings that they do not exist separately in their own right as persons with freedom of their own. Rather, he contends that existential approaches that speak more of the synthesis of the identity of the persons are more effective.

The pastor can appropriate the foregoing insights in the following ways: First, he can assume without fear of being too wrong that many of the people he meets daily are struggling, not to win arguments, but to survive as a personal existence of their own. They will retreat into isolation when pastor *or* doctor treats them as *things* rather than persons (petrifies them). They react with terror when their personal space—however lonely it is— is "broken into" or imploded. Whatever else a pastor does, therefore, he must *never crowd the person, fence him in, or badger him.* These approaches may be appropriate in other instances, but in the case of the schizoid, man-without-a-country kind of person spoken of in this chapter, they are never appropriate. Instead, the pastor must slow down, pull back, and measure the distance between this person and his world.

In Summary

The territorial imperative—its denial, frustration, and invasion—provides the assumption of this chapter that healthy religion gives the individual a private "closet" of being and that religion is sick when a person is denied this. The findings of Ardrey, Hall, and May are used as theoretical data and the quests of three persons for their own territory are used as clinical material. Pastoral approaches to persons such as these are discussed, such as the pastor's guardianship of persons' solitude, his evaluation of the sleep routine, his use of sensitivity training, and his ministry of prayer. Correlation of the pastoral approaches with a study from the existential therapists concludes the chapter.

Chapter 6

FORGIVENESS
AND UNFORGIVINGNESS
AND SICK RELIGION

THE LITERATURE on the relationship between religion and
mental illness abounds with references to guilt. It was
Lewis Sherrill who first called to my attention the importance of forgiveness in the face of the dark specter of
guilt in the mentally disturbed person. Sherrill pointed
to factors in psychotherapy that have an especial meaning
for the life of faith and "the deeper appreciation of its
resources by pastor and people." (Lewis Sherrill, *Guilt
and Redemption,* pp. 142 ff.; The John Knox Press, 1945.)
These factors are: the establishing of a personal relationship that treats the person *as* a person; reliving the
person's "own private little hell" with him; acceptance,
or the kind of reconciling forgiveness that casts out fear;
transference, or the learning of how to express both love
and hostility toward the therapist; and rebirth—in that
a previous self passes away, and a new self is born into
being.

Later, the whole field of psychiatry and religion became
indebted to David Roberts for an understanding of forgiveness as the antidote for the sense of guilt. Roberts
described a theistic faith as being in "the language of

drama and personal relation—struggle and triumph, anxiety and fellowship, guilt and forgiveness." (David Roberts, *Psychotherapy and a Christian View of Man*, p. 87; Charles Scribner's Sons, 1950.) Such release from guilt through forgiveness can result in a transformation of the self. This happens in psychotherapy when one faces and grasps "the deeply hidden causes of inner dividedness." (*Ibid.*, p. 135.) One receives acceptance (i.e., forgiveness).

More recently, E. Mansell Pattison, M.D., has elucidated the problem of guilt and forgiveness by distinguishing between ego morality and superego morality. On the one hand, superego morality is more childish, more compulsive, and more determined by one's previous history; on the other hand, ego morality is more responsible, more related to present reality, and more free in its power of personal decision. Pattison says that psychoanalysts such as Hartmann, Rapaport, and Erikson have "systematically elaborated the role of so-called autonomous ego function." (E. Mansell Pattison, "Morality, Guilt, and Forgiveness," *International Psychiatry Clinic*, Vol. 5, No. 4, p. 100; Little, Brown and Company, 1969.) In another place he states the recent developments among ego psychologists as follows:

> Although couched in various terms, there is a growing consensus that personality development reflects not only physiological needs, but also value needs. Such needs to "make sense out of the world" have been termed the "quasi-needs" of the ego (von Bertalanffy), the will to meaning (Frankl), ego efficacy (White), and cognitive coherence (Festinger). . . .

These autonomous ego functions assume the function of "ego drives" in contradistinction to "instinctual drives." These ego drives are dependent upon the beliefs and values of the culture and these drives become important if indeed not the overriding determinants of behavior. Thus it can be seen that belief systems or value systems are the data that the ego uses to organize individual behavior. The lack of such cultural value data results in the failure to develop an effective coherent ego structure; or the cultural value system may result in significant distortions in the formation of ego structure. Belief systems, whether they be religious or otherwise, then are both necessary and influential in the development of personality. (E. Mansell Pattison, *The Effects of a Religious Culture's Values on Personality Psychodynamics;* American Association for the Advancement of Science, Berkeley, California, 1965.)

In the course of his formulations, Pattison classifies four kinds of guilt that provide the "stuff" of forgiveness and unforgivingness. He speaks, first, of an arbitrary and impersonal guilt, which he calls "civil guilt" or the breaking of specific laws. Then he describes, second, psychological, subjective guilt *feelings,* or the internal effect of self-condemnation. Existential guilt is the third kind that springs from the interaction between man and man. People are estranged from each other, as in the case of divorce. Some guilt attends this estrangement in most instances. Finally, Pattison speaks of ontological guilt and says that this, theologically speaking, is original sin. It is that "fatal flaw of human character that leads man to damn himself." (*Clinical Psychiatry and Religion,* p. 105.) Pattison observes:

In terms of ego morality, the question is not one of guilt but rather of the assessment of what one is and how one behaves in order that one may modify one's behavior in terms of one's conscious moral commitments. (*Ibid.*, p. 107.)

Pattison rejects the "punitive model" for forgiveness such as a superego or narcissistic model of forgiveness would demand in terms of "appeasement, restitution, paying back or making up" for wrongdoing. Rather, he proposes a "reconciliation model of forgiveness." (E. Mansell Pattison, "On the Failure to Forgive or to Be Forgiven," *American Journal of Psychotherapy,* Vol. 19, 1965, p. 106.) By this he means that one is "learning to accept oneself when one realizes that one is unacceptable; and seeking reconciliation from the estrangement one's behavior has brought." Pattison defines forgiveness by saying that the need for forgiveness is filled with "anxiety." "The anxiety is not over punishment but estrangement; the driving force for the resolution of guilt is the deprivation of love. . . . Here the process of forgiveness is that of reconciliation in the I-Thou of love." (*Ibid.*, p. 107.)

Pattison's model of forgiveness is the ideal one of which Paul Tillich speaks in describing faith as the "courage to be," i.e., of accepting that one is accepted by God even though one is unacceptable to one's self.

Therefore, my hypothesis in this chapter is that religion becomes sick when a person is unwilling and/or unable to appropriate the forgiveness of God and his fellowman or is unwilling and/or unable to forgive those from whom he is estranged. He erects a wall of unforgiv-

ingness around himself that isolates him from his "significant others," with whom he must live. The publican is
an example of the self-condemnatory model of forgiveness as appeasement, atonement rituals, and repetition
compulsions. The elder brother who was "angry, and
would not go in" to celebrate the return of the prodigal
is an example of the unforgiving person who withdraws
into a persecutory shell and continues to do so even when
no real damage has been done him at all. The kind of
sick religion involved in both such instances is apparent
as a garden variety of ambulatory sick people who never
get to physicians for treatment or to pastors for the
ministry of confession and absolution. Yet the symptoms
on top of the unresolved guilt consist of reaction formations such as exceptional religious zealotry that "breathes
threatenings and slaughters" against the "heretic," the
repetition of confessions of small infractions of cultural
taboos around them, and *exceptional* preoccupation with
abstract philosophical doctrines to the detriment of those
around them. Another example of these garden varieties
of sick religion is found in the compulsive church worker
who spends the majority of his waking hours in activistic
church "doing." It is as if he does and does and does *in
order* to be accepted and approved in spite of the fact
that he does not accept himself.

Recently the Group for the Advancement of Psychiatry
published a monograph entitled *The Psychic Function of
Religion in Mental Illness and Health.* In the tradition
of a kind of psychoanalysis that puts much stress on the
development and defense of the ego, the authors publish
an intriguing case history of a "Methodical Methodist,"
which reflects a ropelike braiding of both unforgiveness
and unforgivingness in the themes of the man's life. I

quote by permission the case and its interpretation in its entirety as follows:

On the eve of his appointment to a professorship in an American university, a highly moral 40-year-old college teacher, then engaged in scholarly pursuits at Oxford University, impulsively picked up a prostitute on the streets of London. No sooner had he left her than he developed a consuming, paralyzing, guilt-laden fear of syphilis and insanity. Later he became afraid of murdering someone in his family, and got rid of an ax out of the fear that he might use it involuntarily. Feeling like an unworthy sinner, he became agitated and depressed, unable either to sleep or to carry on his work. He wished to be hospitalized and wondered whether castration might alleviate his symptoms.

The patient was a solemn scholar, a professor of history who specialized in 18th-century England. His considerable energies were almost completely devoted to his work, and his pleasures were in the main derived from it. The English accent of his deep, stentorian voice was sometimes broken—but only during times of acute stress—by a weak Southern drawl. The gestures of his hands were those of an orator. Hard work was the keynote of his life. He had published many learned articles and books and edited others, and was a bibliographer of note. At intervals, he took count of the number of pages in his *oeuvres*. He made meticulous use of his time, rising at 5 A.M. daily and thereafter going through his routine chores according to a prescribed formula. Activities that took him away from his work provoked anxiety on his part. He was frugal, far more so than his financial position demanded. He felt it immoral to squander money, but he also feared being left penniless if he did so. The exception to his frugality was the purchase of books, and he was proud of his extensive, well-ordered library.

He was scrupulously proper, not only as a scholar and teacher, but also in his daily dealings with family, friend, and stranger alike. He was a popular teacher; his courses were organized with precision and presented dramatically and articulately. A sense of humor, usually absent from his activities in other areas, sometimes came to light in his classes. He was strict, however, in adhering to the rules and demanded high standards both from his pupils and from colleagues of lesser rank. In spite of severe anxieties, he enjoyed addressing large classes and remained composed under classroom stress. His hobby was the study of foreign languages, and he was fluent in several. He greatly enjoyed travel and study in foreign countries. In contrast to his punctuality, punctiliousness, and propriety, he dressed carelessly; his clothes tended to be unpressed, unclean, or unbuttoned.

He was envious and critical of older colleagues although invariably polite in their presence. On the other hand, he was gracious and helpful in his dealings with students. He was ambitious not only as a teacher and scholar, but also as an administrator. This split loyalty occasioned much distress on his part. While he sought to be with distinguished, intelligent, famous, and wealthy people, he was uncomfortable in their presence.

He was concerned with the underdog and voiced liberal views on such issues as race discrimination and security for the poor and sick. Yet he was conservative in regard to the loosening of social and sexual restrictions on youth, or the modernization of educational rules. He resented passionately those who, he felt, exploited him or others; physicians in private practice who milked the sick and the poor led the list. It was typical for him to react to stress or disappointment by working harder than ever; success in work helped alleviate the discomfort.

He had married prudently. To him, his wife's chief

characteristic was the fact that she was from a family that was distinguished by its intellect, in addition to being wealthy. The relationship with her, although generally friendly, had little warmth or intimacy. Sexual relations were routine, and lacked spontaneity; during them, he frequently fantasied himself in an orgy with a "promiscuous slut." Fantasies of this sort often stressed the buttocks.

Both as boy and man, he did not utter obscene words and felt uncomfortable when others did so. His rich, though disturbing inner life included the fantasy of being a distinguished Englishman, such as a statesman, a duke, or a Lord Admiral. His dreams frequently had to do with the toilet, soiling, and bowel movements. He also had "snob dreams," set in plush surroundings where he consorted with royalty or presidents. Though he had not attained the peak of his fantasies, he considered himself to be extraordinarily lucky and feared that it would all disappear in an instant.

Early Life and Development

The professor was born in Georgia. Early in life he developed an intense shame about himself, his parents, and his Southern origin. His mother he described as crippled, uneducated, and shrewish; her family had more than its share of mental instability and insanity. He suspected that she had Negro blood and that he himself was "contaminated" with it. This fear was intensified by the fact that his dark complexion and black hair resembled hers. He was less ashamed of his father, although ill at ease with his vulgarity and his drawl; he was pleased, however, that some of his father's ancestors had come from England. He became suspicious of his parents at an early age, probably five, when they did not celebrate their wedding anniversary; he feared that he, the firstborn, had

been conceived out of wedlock. When he was 11, he confirmed this suspicion.

He described himself as a "very unsuccessful little boy."
He had been expected to die during an attack of measles
at the age of 18 months; thereafter, he was treated as a
frail, sickly child. He was frightened by fellow students,
from whose physical abuse his younger sister sometimes
protected him. From the age of six on, he had attacks in
which he feared dying of a horrible disease.

His suspicions about his mother's premarital pregnancy
and supposed Negro blood seemed to have fanned the
flames of his sexual lust for her at an early age. Fear,
however, caused him to turn his back upon this temptation and instead he identified himself with her. The
identification was encouraged by the fact that they shared
the same dark features and were both "sick people." It
was further encouraged when he was eight years old, at
which time he injured his penis and went to her for
consolation. Strange as it may seem, she advised him to
watch out for enlargement of his breasts!

The identification with his mother did not completely
repress competitive, murderous feelings toward his father.
These feelings were, however, displaced onto superiors,
whom he often found reason to hate. He dreamed frequently of murder; murderous impulses, as we have seen,
returned during his adult illness.

Self-images included being a "sissy," a "nigger," and a
"bastard." He considered both his head and penis to be
abnormally small, but he often gazed with pride at the
size of his bowel movement. He felt stupid, and from the
beginning did poorly in school. His first-grade teacher
warned him that he was incapable of learning.

Intense anal-erotic and anal-sadistic impulses, in part a
regressive defense against genital impulses, added to his
feelings of shame and guilt. He had been thoroughly

toilet-trained at an early age, and was regarded as an eager-to-please, sweet boy. Erotic feelings centered around his anus; he often dreamed of soiling, toilets, and large piles of refuse, which symbolized feces. His earliest erotic memories concerned his uncle's buttocks, cut off from the body. In childhood, his sexual interest concerned itself more with a girl's buttocks than with her genitals. Anal messiness spread to other functions; his school-papers were criticized as untidy and his thinking as muddled. Later on, he developed reaction-formations to this messiness; he recorded data and assembled information with great care, and his thinking became meticulous. This combination of anal impulse and reaction-formation contributed to his amassing of a large bibliography, which contributed to his success.

In part out of the need to assuage oedipal guilt, and in part in order to regain an imagined infancy in which he had come to be loved through being ill and dying, he was already a masochistic hypochondriac at the age of six. At the same time, he developed masochistic fantasies, in one of which he was mortally ill, and his grieving mother was sitting at his side. Before dying, he turned black, as if to remind her what her imagined Negro ancestry had visited on him. In another, he was a servant, imprisoned in the stall of a public toilet, being tortured in order to entertain a princess.

When the boy was ten, the father became exasperated with his weakness and hypochondriasis and commanded him to "be a man." In response, he began to exercise regularly, forced himself out of isolation, and experimented with his voice, which soon deepened. He thought of outdoing his father's wishes for him: not only would he "be a man," but he would be a great one at that. Every night he prayed, "May I be a truly great man." The shame he felt toward himself and family spread to his

house and neighborhood. He yearned for the life of a
Southern gentleman, full of dignity.

Religious Background

The members of his family were devout Southern
Methodists. His maternal grandfather was an itinerant
preacher. The future scholar faithfully attended the
church, its Sunday school, and its other functions. It was
the one unifying influence of childhood. *There* he felt
accepted, and the emotional atmosphere of its revival
meetings stirred him deeply.

The repeated warnings against sin and about the need
to prepare for death, however, frightened him. Guilt and
masochism, the latter derived in part from the childhood
bout with death, made Hell seem fearfully close. But the
solution to the problems that his churchgoing underscored for him was also provided by the church: hard
work. Life was represented as a testing period for the
beyond, and work was the key to acceptance in Heaven.
Further, working one's fingers to the bone satisfied some
masochistic needs. His Methodist teaching led him to
regard the Bible as a library of great literature, the
nucleus out of which his religion had grown. This attitude contributed toward an intense desire to read the
Bible and understand it. This interest soon spread to
other literature, thus laying the foundation for his evolution into a scholar. The warm, emotional atmosphere of a
revivalist church gave some outlet to his erotic feelings, in
addition to the promise that high morals and hard work
would guarantee the satisfaction of his dependent wishes,
whether on earth or in Heaven.

Latency—Elijah and Christ. During latency, he was
especially impressed by the Bible stories about Elijah and
Christ. Partial identification with each of them helped
lighten some conflicts. He consciously fantasied himself as

Elijah, who had outlawed the worship of Ba'al, with its vulgar and licentious orgies, and had encouraged instead the return to a more austere religion. He had literally thrown the immoral Jezebel to the dogs. In identifying himself with Elijah, the boy sought to eliminate his own wicked desires and to find a key character defense—austerity. At the same time, the wicked Jezebel, whom he equated with his mother, was to be removed as an object of temptation. Elijah's miracles inspired him, especially the one in which Elijah raised the widow's son from the dead, for he too had been miraculously snatched from death! Elijah's final dramatic departure to Heaven in a chariot of fire swept by a whirlwind was a proud exit indeed for a "dirty nigger bastard," who might otherwise have been expected to drop straight into Hell! Both miracles helped fan omnipotent feelings that relieved him of his shame.

He viewed Christ as a New Testament reincarnation of Elijah: Christ too brought the dead back to life. Christ also helped him see that sins can be forgiven and showed him how to work out masochistic fantasies in a socially acceptable way. It is not certain whether the *Pietà* fantasy of dying in the presence of a grieving mother facilitated the identification with Christ or resulted from it. He became a Christ who took on the sins of the world—a neat way of rationalizing his feelings of being a sinner. If a classmate erred, he confessed and took the punishment. Literary inclinations, already fanned by an interest in the Bible, centered on the fantasy of writing a book about a boy's suffering. This book would bring him fame.

Adolescence and John Wesley. As he entered adolescence, these identity components became less satisfying. The emotional atmosphere and the magical ideas brought him too close to the loss of control he feared. The shame that he felt for himself and his family contaminated his attitude toward the local church. But there was someone in the church to whom he could turn—John Wesley. He had long been acquainted with Wesley, the 18th-century founder of Methodism. When he was 11 years old, his grandmother had given him a book of Wesley's sermons. Wesley was venerated in the church, and the growing boy put him above Jesus. Wesley proved to be a more practical source for finding solutions to his adolescent dilemmas than did the Biblical figures. His interest in Wesley continued even after he left the church: he wrote a term paper about Wesley in high school, and would probably have made Wesley the topic of his Ph.D. thesis, had he not been afraid that this would mark him as a Southern Methodist.

Wesley, who shared his initials, had preached in Georgia for several years, and it was easy for the adolescent to imagine himself following in the great man's footsteps. Wesley, like him, had been a sickly child but had blossomed into a vigorous and successful man, perhaps the most energetic of his day; to be like him would more than fill the father's demand that he "be a man." Wesley was an English gentleman who traced his pedigree back to a 10th-century nobleman. His father was the Anglican rector of Epworth and a man of letters; his mother, the daughter of a vicar and related to an earl. Her training is said to have formed the foundation of Wesley's character. The adolescent boy felt that his own mother, by contrast, was largely responsible for the shame he felt about himself. To be Wesley and to have such a mother, even in fantasy, would be to undo his destiny. To a boy who regarded himself as a low Southerner, in being a Wesley he would surpass even the hitherto envied Southern gentleman. Indeed he would be a distinguished English gentleman, accent included.

Wesley had given up a social life at Oxford in order

to become an ascetic preacher. As a preacher, he was a spellbinder, imperturbable in front of a crowd. He was rigid in belief and action, and lived by hard work. Methodism originated in the methodical conduct for which Wesley was himself the model. He was precise and punctilious, both in worship and in the practice of life. He rose every morning at 4:00 A.M., and carefully noted his activities in a daily journal; he was frugal and led a simple life. The boy was thus given leave to give up the social life that had been forced upon him by his father. Once having decided to follow directly in Wesley's footsteps by becoming a minister, he isolated himself from his peers and ascended in fantasy to a preacher's pulpit, from which he could look down on the crowd, instead of feeling looked down upon by them. Erotic and hostile feelings were partially controlled by this fantasy, although hostility could continue to be expressed in righteous indignation against sinners. In his later identity as a professor, he simply converted the pulpit into a podium and carried Wesley's composure as a preacher into the classroom. The whining weakling became an effective, full-voiced orator. Like Wesley, he arose early in the morning (although not until 5:00 A.M.), maintained punctilious study habits, and kept a journal. The shame-laden frugality and simple life that had been forced on him in childhood by his economic and social status had now become the admirable attributes of a moral and genteel man.

To the future professor, as well as in reality, Wesley had been much more than the founder of Methodism. He was a scholar, a literary man, a teacher, and an expert in foreign languages, as well as a writer, translator, editor, and traveler. From college on, the professor gradually managed to include all these interests in his own identity. The boy who had been told in the primary grades that he could not learn and who had struggled through high school became an honor student in college and was graduating magna cum laude. Wesley had encouraged the publication of inexpensive books in order to create a popular taste for good reading, and the professor associated this with the large accumulation of paperbacks in his library.

Wesley's preaching had been directed toward "the unclean beasts"; he ministered to the humble and the poor, exorcising the greedy clergy who were interested only in parishioners with wealth and position. Hence his mission to Georgia. He fought against slavery and was one of the first in England to promote medical clinics for the poor. In contrast to these activities, he was also a high churchman and a Tory. At first, the humble Southern boy felt protected by Wesley, the venerated churchman; later, however, he identified himself with Wesley's humanitarianism and promoted human rights. His hatred for the South's treatment of Negroes, while a part of this humanistic attitude, was also a means of expressing anger about his own feared origin. Wesley severely criticized the physicians of his time and opened medical clinics for the poor. The professor's contempt for the greedy doctors who prospered on the suffering of others barely repressed his wish to be a greedy patient himself, who would be forever entitled to care and protection. In this respect, Wesley became for him a protecting parent rather than an object for identification. Without any financial need to do so, he often considered transferring from private care to a public clinic. Wesley was an outstanding administrator of his flock, as well as a scholar and teacher; the professor's administrative ambitions, by contrast, while partially successful, caused him anguish, for he did not have enough time for all of these activities. Further, his serious, rigid temperament was not acceptable to a liberal faculty, which was intent on maintaining its academic freedom.

He also unconsciously imitated Wesley's less successful aspects. Wesley did not offer the youth a satisfying model for relating to women, for his own love life had been far from happy. He had been forced to break off an imprudent relationship with a woman in Georgia. Love had been lacking in his marriage; ultimately, his wife had left him. The professor was more fortunate than Wesley in his marriage partner; but to him the marriage was essentially a prudent alliance, and lacked warmth and intimacy.

Adult Identity

The identity of the professor was not a mere composite of the identity elements he took on from the Methodist Church and his successive identifications with the religious figures attached to it. The partial identifications with Elijah and Christ helped tide him through the latency period, but they were barely discernible in his adult identity; except for Elijah's austerity, which had been reinforced by Wesley's austerity, they existed mainly in omnipotent and masochistic fantasy. Wesley, however, played a leading role in it, especially in its ego-syntonic aspects. Yet the professor was no Wesley: he could not cope with the problem of being a real preacher, for to do so would have tied him to the Southern Methodist Church and to his Southern origins, a tie that was too painful for him to continue. Also the magical ideas that are inherent in religious myths threatened his cherished reason, which was so important in shielding him from the fear of insanity. In specializing in the 18th century, the professor's fantasy life had been focused on Wesley's era; yet this had also been the Age of Reason. While being a preacher did not solve the

dilemma, his identity as an English scholar and teacher
—an important segment of Wesley's identity—had enabled him to carry on the Wesley identification in a practical and satisfying fashion. In finding his way, he had
formed partial identifications with a succession of literary
and historical figures, as well as with his own college pro-
fessors. This had enabled him to scale himself down to
the proportions that his own talents and environment
would permit him actually to achieve, instead of blindly
attempting to mimic the never-to-be-achieved ideal of
his adored god, Wesley.

Failure of Identity and Symptom Formation

The integration of talents, drives, defenses, identifications, and environment did not result in a fully satisfying whole. Much of his shame and guilt remained
unbound, and not enough of his hope and pride was able
to become bound, in the identity of the professor. The
low Southerner and the compensatory Great Man both
lingered in the background, while the wished-for ideal
of the professor came closer and closer to being realized.
In the scholarly Oxonian England that he loved and that
he shared in fantasy with John Wesley, at the moment
when he was preparing to enter into a professorship to
which he had long aspired, he was threatened with the
possibility of success. The unbound shame and guilt,
on the other hand, led to a fear of failure. The idea that
dream and reality were so close together caused his
latent fear of insanity to burst into the open. For him,
to become insane meant that his anal sadistic and murderous oedipal thoughts would come into consciousness
and be acted upon; on the other hand, there was the
danger that the delusion of being a Wesley or one of the
other Great Men after whom he had patterned himself
might emerge full-blown. These fears drove him to act out

two more or less repressed identity components: that of the sexual reprobate and that of the helpless patient. The tremendous control over his instincts that had led him to the brink now gave way to reenactment of oedipal fantasies with the London prostitute, who reminded him of the image of his mother—low and sexually promiscuous. But as a helpless patient, he returned to a protecting, preoedipal cradle, thereby avoiding the possibility of adult failure. For failure meant that he would be forced to return, Cinderella-like, to his ignoble origins.

The case presented above illustrates the fact that characterological derivatives of church affiliation relate only in part to religious doctrines themselves, or to the "religious" qualities of its leaders or prophets. Factors that are more or less irrelevant to the religious message may play an equally significant role. Psychoanalytic studies cannot draw clear lines between doctrinal aspects and seemingly incidental aspects—a reflection of the fact that the unconscious cannot do so either. The particular aspects of religion that are utilized by one individual, as well as the particular uses that he makes of them in character formation, depend on what he brings to religion from previous development and present conflict, and from the ensemble of his liabilities, assets, and needs.

As this case study shows, the religious material in psychoanalysis may not be manifestly religious. On the other hand, manifest religious content may have little to do with the influence of religion. A particular gesture or tone of voice may have originated in a significant religious experience, whereas a long discussion of church activities may have little significance. Knowledge of latent content is as essential here as it is in the study of dreams.

Religious figures and religious myths are sometimes said to be projections. The individual may perceive them, not as they exist in the mind of the theologian nor as they are described in the Bible or by the pastor, but as extensions of his own private world. From this point of view, he makes his own religion. Are we then to conclude that such religious ideation, psychologically speaking, is merely adapted to carry on one's previous relationships and identifications, along with the conflicts associated with them? That happens, but, as we can see in the case of the professor, something else happens too. The individual may perceive qualities that are not projections, but that nonetheless fill specific needs or answer specific problems for him at a particular time. These qualities may then add a new essence to living. (*The Psychic Function of Religion in Mental Illness and Health,* Vol. VI, No. 67, pp. 690–702; Group for the Advancement of Psychiatry, 1968. Used by permission of the publisher.)

My own interpretation of this case points up my hypothesis about sick religion. In the first place, the "Methodical Methodist" could not feel accepted as who he was in fact. He focused most of his self-rejection upon his birthplace and parents, facts and persons who permit of no substitution. Erik Erikson says that maturity can be said to consist of accepting one's parents and origins as nonnegotiable and permitting of no substitution.

The only alternative to this kind of forgiveness extended to one's own heritage is a life of repetitious *undoing* of the facts and persons of one's heritage. This kind of "Out, damned spot!" behavior consistently appeared in the life of the Methodical Methodist. In his inability to forgive and be reconciled with his parents, he remained estranged, alienated, and alone. His symptom formation revealed his kinship with the "low and sexually promiscuous" life he attributed—rightly or not—to his mother. It was a kind of private ritual of confession, an attempt to communicate with conscious intention the ambivalent lack of forgiveness and search for punishment of which neurosis is made. In one and the same act, he both confessed his inability to forgive and received punishment for atonement in his role as a sick patient. He, as the authors of the case suggest, got the status of a sick person and the exemption from any responsibility for his own acts.

In the second place, the case materials show vividly the *uses* to which religion is put in the individual's struggle for survival as an independent self. The man rebelled against what he considered to be a sordid and ignorant background. The case material is weakly presented in that the details of the religious instruction of the man are not known or not given. We do not know the data about the religious ideas, behavior, and emotions of the parents. Familiarity with the kind of culture in which the man grew up prompts one to hazard a guess that the parents were not religious at all or were extremely religious. I prefer to assume that the disdain the man expresses indicates that the parents were irreligious and uneducated skilled laborers at best. They probably wanted their son to have what they were deprived of—an education. The education, in turn, alienated him from them and was rationalized through the intellectualisms of his education, his use of language in writing, and his moral superiority feelings about himself in contradistinction from them. The alienation itself produced a burden of unresolved guilt, which in turn manifested itself in his sick behavior and religion. His fastidiousness belied his heritage of uncouthness.

In the third place, the case history shows that the man's awareness that he was born out of wedlock was a primordial source of feelings of being unwanted. These feelings seem to reflect, in addition to unforgivingness toward his parents, a feeling of *being unforgiven and unblessed by his parents*. They did not celebrate their wedding anniversary. Apparently, they would have been even less likely to celebrate *his birthday*. He, in a sense, was a blot on the family escutcheon. He entered life disfranchised.

Neither do we find any data about his siblings in the history. If he, as the firstborn, did not have the welcoming blessing of his parents, was there another sibling upon whom their approval *was* lavished to the exclusion of the patient? As long as Biblical figures of identification are being used in the interpretation, one asks about the siblings to see if there is a Cain and an Abel, a Jacob and an Esau, a Joseph and his elder brothers, or a prodigal son and an elder brother. I have noticed how quick analysts are to use father-child and mother-child symbols from the Scriptures and how sibling rivalry and religious-educational motivation are a part of each other. In short, was there, in addition to a "black-mother" image that haunted the patient, a "black sheep" of a sibling that followed him as well. Could he *dare* to be as profligate as his brother, for instance, without losing the approval of his parents?

Finally, the illness of the man represents an invasion

of *his* territory by the reenactment of his memories of his heritage apart from his own personal control. Here is how ontological guilt can be the fatal flaw of human character whereby the sins of the fathers are visited on the children unto the third and fourth generations. The purpose of effective religion is not to reenforce the reaction formations of an *utterly* discontinuous and *completely* different life in the young as opposed to that of their parents. Rather, effective religion enables the ego functions of the growing youth to reappraise the strengths as well as the weaknesses of his heritage and to lower the emotional importance of one's earthly family to realistic levels. Thus the new territory established by the young "scribe," as the Methodical Methodist was in fact, will include things *both* old and new. This, as has been said before, is the interpretation Freud himself gave of the psychic function of religion in mental illness and health. Freud's comment in essence was that the function of religion in the mental health of a person, ideally, was to lower the importance of the earthly family, to give the individual's instinctive strivings a safe ethical mooring place, and to enable him to have access to the larger family of mankind. If the above patient's religion could have been such as to have lowered the intensity of his involvement with his earthly parents, then it could be said to have been a well and not a sick religion. As it was it was sick. This idea of Freud's, regretfully, does not appear in the report of the Group for the Advancement of Psychiatry. (For further reference read Sigmund Freud, *Collected Papers,* Vol. III, 2d ed., p. 597.) Lowering "the importance of one's earthly family," however, does not mean the denying of one's family as having *any* importance. In *Christ and Selfhood,* I pointed out that in the life of Jesus the paradoxical process went on as he freed himself of his family—both parents and siblings—and as he unabashedly proclaimed his new identity in his hometown of Nazareth. This paradox, in one way or another, produces either a creative or destructive tension in the religious and intellectual pilgrimage of men and women who in fact do grow and achieve a place or a territory in life that is uniquely their own.

THERAPY AND UNFORGIVENESS

One of the real gaps in the presentation of the case of the Methodical Methodist is the absence of any discussion of the therapeutic process of caring for the patient. One leaves the case material wishing for this. In order to focus well upon this dimension of the present discussion, I am presenting a second case prepared by Theodore Bonstedt, M.D. The emphasis of this case is upon the positive role of religion in the treatment of a psychiatric patient in that patient's movement toward recovery. I present it as is and will then make some pastoral observations. The aim of this chapter is to understand what the "private hell" of the patient is like. Techniques of the confessional ministry can be found elsewhere (Max Thurian, *Confession;* London: SCM Press, Ltd., 1959. Wayne E. Oates, *Protestant Pastoral Counseling,* pp. 89–91, 184–185; The Westminster Press, 1964). The concern here is with counselor insight, which is always a tedious process to develop. The following case report makes specific the positive values of confession and confrontation in the recovery of a psychiatric patient:

Against this historical background, let us consider the situation of a white, Protestant, 31-year-old married man who was referred to us for psychiatric treatment in the summer of 1960. He was very anxious, almost panicky, as he could not stop himself from vivid sexual fantasies and actions. He was spending long periods of time walking the streets of his city, following a particular "pair of shapely feminine legs"; he would follow up this activity by much masturbation and abuse of his wife, whom he would openly accuse of not being well-built enough to satisfy his sexual needs. Then again there were recurrent moments of despair, a realization that he was immoral and sinning, but many confessions and discussions with his minister would not break this cycle. His worry and anxiety had increased to the point where for much of the time it was no longer possible to concentrate upon his work as an accountant.

The background of this man was unusually traumatic. His mother had been known as a manic-depressive psychotic patient even prior to the birth of our patient. The father was described by the professional people who knew the family as "nearly psychotic," a strict disciplinarian. Although the patient's older sister tried to serve as a "substitute mother," there was often little she could do when the mother was violent, banging her head against the wall, running and screaming around the house for hours at a time, in fact trying to kill the patient by choking him on at least two well-documented occasions. As the sister became older, she tried to protect our patient from the parental outbursts by taking him into bed with her whenever she heard him stir at night. When the patient was 12, his father died after an operation for a malignant growth, and shortly afterward his mother was committed to a nearby State Hospital for long-term care. The mother died in the State Hospital

some years later, but while she stayed there she continued
to have various bizarre ideas, and so she told the patient's
older sister that her son wanted to abuse her (the mother)
sexually.

The patient was first referred to a psychiatrist at the
age of 18 after a fight with his mother. As usual, he
threatened that he would "go out with bad women,"
which seemed to be the only way that he could really
get back at his mother. He was then hospitalized for
six months because of what his hospital record describes
as "a psychotic illness with catatonic agitation." He was
treated with deep sleep and psychotherapy, then was
followed for three years on an outpatient basis, after
which (1951) he was seen only once or twice a year.
Meanwhile his performance improved to the point where
he was employed steadily and efficiently at a local corpora-
tion. He married a shy, reticent young woman, and soon
started many arguments over how inadequate she was
as a sexual partner, not having enough size to her bust
or any sufficient proportions otherwise. In spite of this,
he remained very attached to his children, was a good
provider, and was regularly practicing his Protestant
religion.

In 1959 (at the age of 28) our patient was asked to
leave town on a business trip, as part of a promotion on
his job. There followed much anxiety, insomnia, an-
orexia; outpatient treatment by the previous doctor
proved insufficient and he was rehospitalized. He was
treated with phenothiazines and psychotherapy. Although
he seemed to improve and was discharged in two weeks,
he had to be readmitted because of an increase in the
previous symptoms five days after discharge. He was
described by his doctor as "feeling unwanted, with a
feminine identification, with much sibling rivalry toward
his younger brother." On this third psychiatric hospitali-

zation (which was actually a continuation of the second), since even rather high doses of Trilafon (8 mg. q.i.d.) would not make him more comfortable, a course of 10 electro-convulsive treatments was undertaken. His anxiety diminished and he was followed as an outpatient with tranquilizing medication and psychotherapy by a psychologist. The diagnosis during the second and third hospitalizations was psychoneurosis, anxiety reaction.

The patient's therapist left the city early in 1960, and it was felt that the patient probably would not need further psychotherapy. However, a few weeks prior to our evaluation of him in the summer of 1960, the above-mentioned obsession with not getting enough sexual pleasure returned; once more he was very anxious, almost panicky, pleading for help to prevent another psychiatric hospitalization. At this time we were impressed with the extent of the traumata suffered by this man, and by the 12-year history of a successively psychotic and then neurotic disorder. Under the circumstances it did not appear that further application of a conventional psychoanalytically oriented psychotherapy would offer much hope. We felt that some sort of "synthetical" approach was indicated instead, based upon some asset or strength already present within this man. Since his social history and his own verbal production in the interview were replete with references to an apparently genuine religious faith, decision was made to use this religious conviction as a lever or pivot from which to start a new chapter in the man's rehabilitation at this critical time. Accordingly, after he stated that some of his previous doctors were permissive toward the idea of his trying out a prostitute, he was somewhat surprised when, instead, we posed the question (in the very first hour of psychotherapy) whether or not he wished to remain a man whose utmost goal is that of greatest sexual pleasure.

We explained to the patient that apparently he had never questioned this point, taking for granted the feeling that he had to be sure of maximum obtainable comfort and pleasure the rest of his days, and that it was an unbearable thought to him that perhaps sometime in the future his wife might not look even as pleasant to him as she did then, and he might indeed feel that he had missed a great deal of sexual experience in the course of his life. The patient at first looked baffled and stunned by this question, then rather impetuously assured me that he wanted to change, but he shifted the topic of conversation. In the next therapy session he reported that he had managed to have a few more relaxed moments when looking at a girl who tempted him by her appearance, as he thought about our discussion and his inclination to surrender the sexual goal. However, it became apparent that his reasoning was that "he did not desire to go out with her because religion says so," and the more he thought in this way, the more the old upsetting thoughts came back. Accordingly, we impressed upon him again the issue of his own decision, his own personal "gamble," rather than what he was told to do. Was his sexual play the most important goal for him by his own decision, or was it not? He momentarily said that it was. We then suggested that in line with this goal it would be only expected that he would drop his wife. He retorted that this was impossible, and we asked what stopped him. With tears in his eyes he confessed that it was the belief in God and also the love for his wife and children.

An interpretation was made that he had been keeping together within his heart two goals which were quite contrary to each other, as if it were possible to keep these two goals at the same time; he was now finding out the hard way that it was quite impossible, that it "was tearing him apart" and that it brought on all the terrible nervous problems. The suggestion was made that, even if the nervous problems had not arisen at all, he surely would have wanted to straighten out such a mess in his life when he found out about it. During the next several hours in psychotherapy, the working-through of this issue was continued, with the patient somewhat undecided. Meanwhile there was more information concerning the very troubled relationship with his wife.

In the fourth hour the patient announced that he had decided he was going to live for the sake of his children and not for the sake of sexual pleasure above all. Curiously enough, the patient tried to place partial blame upon two psychiatrists and one psychologist previously involved with him, who reportedly encouraged him to practice extramarital sex "to help himself," since otherwise "suppression is going to take revenge on him." His preoccupation with obtaining pleasure was interpreted as having to do partly with his traumatic background, where on so many occasions it seemed he had been "cheated out of something" which other children obtained naturally.

With the patient's permission, we started seeing his wife on some occasions, jointly as well as separately, as many episodes of his panic appeared to have a direct connection with interaction in marriage. As the wife herself confirmed, the patient, for the first time in his life, became really concerned about her as a person, being now motivated to make up for some of his previous neglect of her and the children.

Throughout this time the patient made frequent references to his group meetings in "Recovery" and his counseling sessions with his minister, the latter being placed within the framework of a strictly spiritual counseling (both of these activities had been going on for years).

The patient made spontaneous comments on how the
approach taken by us was particularly helpful in that
there was no disagreement or conflict with his religious
teaching. Thus he found himself able to apply his religious teaching more consciously and more consistently.
Although throughout the first year of psychotherapy
there were many brief returns of panic during which
rehospitalization seemed imminent, he was in fact hospitalized only once for a month in the fall of 1961, following a particularly stressful situation in his job. The
intensity of psychotherapy and the approach used continued unchanged after hospitalization; at this time the
issue of his excessive dependence upon a doctor (most
openly shown in demand for more tranquilizers and
sleeping pills) was finally faced with the assistance of
genetic interpretations and joint sessions with the wife.
Since early 1962 there has been a marked and steady im-
provement in his psychiatric symptoms, coinciding with
his spontaneous verbalization of his chosen values: trying to be a good father and husband rather than getting
the utmost in sexual pleasure, trying to do his best
rather than fulfilling some absolute standard of achieve-
ment, trying to do his best today rather than anticipating
all the future to follow.

As the sexual and aggressive content of the behavior
largely disappeared from the waking life of this man, it
began to appear in his dreams. While during 1962 he was
seen only once a month, in the last three and a half years
he has been seen only two or three times a year, and
these visits coincided with promotions on the job in the
course of which he has successfully traveled as far as a
thousand miles away from home. On such stressful occasions the old sexual thought may reappear briefly, but
there is no more panic, and a brief psychotherapeutic
session is sufficient to tackle the real increased responsi-

bilities. (Theodore Bonstedt, M.D., "Religion as an Asset in a Psychiatric Patient: An Historical and Clinical Comment," *The Journal of Pastoral Care,* Vol. XXII, June, 1968, pp. 84–88. Used by permission.)

PASTORAL OBSERVATIONS

This patient was suffering not only from the symptoms or temptations (if one wishes to think theologically and existentially) that caused him to ask for help in the first place. He defined his problems as sickness and not as in any sense involving his identity as a religious person. He added to the temptation of the sexual fantasies a secondary layer of temptation to make the process of psychiatric treatment a way of life. One wonders if he did not expect the psychiatrists to exorcise his plaguing thoughts with no responsible action on his part at all. Accepting personal responsibility for his acts and thoughts was required of him instead. This realistic confrontation asked that he recognize his behavior, not as something for which he should be punished, but as signs of his alienation from those around him, from himself, and from God. Overcoming this estrangement became the objective of the therapy. Accepting personal responsibility would require that he confess that to some extent he himself had *chosen* this alienation. If he could make a decision about it once, this gave hope that he could make a different decision about it again.

In a sense, psychiatric treatment apart from the assets that religion could offer had produced some side effects of its own. The patient was, as I have said, being tempted to make psychiatric treatment a way of life. To the extent that this had happened, the secondary side effects could be called iatrogenic symptoms. This means that the illness originally called for treatment; then new symptoms appeared as a secondary side effect of the treatment process itself. A simple but clear analogy would be the case of an orthopedic patient suffering multiple fractures from an automobile accident getting bed sores from lying in bed. In this case, Dr. Bonstedt refused to let such an accumulation of problems take place. He focused the patient's sense of guilt upon his responsible relationship to God. This transformed his guilt into a realistic sense of having become alienated from God, i.e., having sinned. Now he was both responsible and being treated as responsible to God for his thinking, saying, and doing. The therapist refused to let the man use the "psychiatric out" from under his sense of responsibility. The therapist did not do this punitively, but in a mood of reconciliation of the two different value systems that were "tearing him apart." The side effect of this was that, inasmuch as he was being treated as a responsible "Thou," he could now place a higher value upon himself. When seen as a responsible "Thou" and not as a petrified collection of symptoms, the man began to act like a responsible human being in his own right.

Ethical Perspective and Sick Religion

The ethical issue at stake in the life of this patient was that of the restoration of the man's personal right and responsibility for decision. The power to decide is a blessing, an affirmation of our humanity, and when it is taken from us we are less than our basic selves. When it is restored, this is acceptance, forgiveness amounting to the reinvestment of trust in us. Yet, this challenges our ambivalence toward either exercising or escaping from the freedom that attends our acceptance of responsibility for making our own decisions. An impressive part of the case report is where Dr. Bonstedt patiently took "several hours in psychotherapy" to work through a moral value issue. The patient was "somewhat undecided." This is the crux of the therapeutic problem—can the therapist "wait out" the forces of indecision and can the patient rise to the occasion of responsible decision on his own? Sherrill speaks of rebirth taking place in psychotherapy. Otto Rank suggests a setting of an end to the therapy by agreeing together with the patient upon a reasonable length of time for "coming through with" some decisions on the part of the patient as to what he intends to be and become. "When he [Otto Rank] did this, he states, he found that the patients began to have birth dreams. The thought of leaving the . . . [therapist], he believed, brought out all the anxieties of birth." (Clara Thompson, M.D., *Psychoanalysis: Evolution and Development,* p. 175; Thomas Nelson & Sons.) Instead of using time to precipitate a decisiveness in this patient, Dr. Bonstedt challenged his relationship to God to become a reality in the processes of his thought.

A reconciliation model for forgiveness is illustrated in this case also. The fantasies that plagued the man were symptomatic of the man's alienation from his wife. He was a religious man but the covenants he made as a husband and a parent stood alongside his behavior as a contradiction, "tearing him apart." The therapy challenged the patient about his estrangement from his wife. His inner territory was closed to his wife. She was, in the course of treatment, involved also. "Room" was made in both their lives for the other to be included. John Bunyan's classical story of the Christian life in *The Pilgrim's Progress* is followed by a less well known writing in which he "goes back" and gets his wife and children and enables them to share in his new life. In a less metaphorical way, psychotherapy was the means of grace whereby the man's wife was "caught up" and "brought into" reconciliation with the husband.

Similarly, the patient as a young adult had not established an effective relationship with a group of his own peers. The "Recovery" group, and his pastor, began to overcome this estrangement, also. Symbolically, the pastor as a person represents the corporate life of the church as a fellowship. In private, he can convey both confrontation and comfort to those who disburden themselves of loads of guilt such as this person expressed. In this way people who would be asocial to the point of pain in the presence of groups of other persons can experience by proxy something of the mind of the group by talking with a pastor.

Paranoid Constructions and Unforgivingness

The patient discussed in the case material above projected much of his problem onto his wife. He held her unforgiven for something about which neither she, himself, nor anyone else could do anything about—her physical form. This relieved him of the responsibility of being accepting of her. There was no chance for her to change the physiognomy of her breasts, etc. Underneath this projection of blame upon his wife was a subtle game going on that relieved him of the responsibility to be adequate as a man in relation to her. Eric Berne would call the game "If It Weren't for You." In rejecting his own humanity, the patient required perfection of others. If it were not forthcoming, he was freed of any responsibility for overcoming the distance between him and his wife.

This, it seems to me, is the dynamic of much paranoid interaction in marriage. (See Wayne E. Oates, "Paranoid Interaction in Marriage," *The Journal of Family Law,* Vol. 4, No. 2, Fall, 1964, pp. 200–208.) The person builds a constellation of complaints against one or more individuals and preoccupation with these relieves him of the responsibility of personal change, understanding, and acceptance of the other person, and, worst of all, keeps a distance between him and other people that is guarded with his whole being.

This, too, is a garden variety of mental illness, which resides at the heart of many church "splits," chronic division among church people, and running battles with a succession of pastors. At best, it is sick religion.

In Summary

The main sources of sick religion rest in the feeling of being unforgiven and the inability to forgive. Various approaches to forgiveness are discussed and the reconciliation model suggested by E. M. Pattison is chosen. The case of the Methodical Methodist is used as illustrative of the dynamic understanding of guilt and shame. The clinical report of a physician on the role of religion as an asset in therapy aims at the matter of pastoral and medical approaches. The possibility of an undesirable set of side effects of a purely psychiatric pattern of treatment that ignores the assets of religion is discussed.

Chapter 7

A PATHOLOGY
OF RELIGIOUS LEADERSHIP

MUCH ATTENTION has been drawn to the role of pathology in the motivation, functioning, and sense of direction of the religious leader. Underlying some of this concern is a *search for validity* of the claims religious leaders have upon the loyalty of their followers, as well as a search for the validity of the truth that they preach. Job is dramatic when he says to Zophar, the Naamathite, and the other "advisers" with him:

> As for you, you whitewash with lies;
> > worthless physicians are you all.
> Oh that you would keep silent,
> > and it would be your wisdom!
> > > > (Job 13:4, 5.)

Both the Judaic and the Christian literature of the Bible reflect awareness of and detailed concern about the sanity and soundness of mind of the leaders of Judaism and Christianity. A brief review of the experiences of Saul, for example, provides good background for the study of a pathology of contemporary leaders of religion.

In I Sam. 16:14 ff., an "evil spirit" is said to have

tormented Saul when the Spirit of the Lord departed from him. The evil spirit was also sent by the Lord. Saul's servants recommended music therapy to free him of the tormenting spirit. David, his later competitor, was a skillful musician with the lyre, "a man of valor, a man of war, prudent in speech, and a man of good presence, and the LORD . . . [was] with him." The musician was as important to the therapy as was the music. David found favor in the sight of Saul: "Saul loved him greatly" and made him his armor-bearer. Through David's music and his presence, "Saul was refreshed, and was well, and the evil spirit departed from him." The narrative speaks of *both* evil spirits *and* illness; Saul became well and free of the evil spirits.

This same Saul became troubled again, as is recorded in I Sam. 28:3–17. Samuel, the spiritual parent who had been Saul's guide for years, had died. Saul had previously "put the mediums and wizards out of the land." In the face of an assault by the Philistine army, Saul resorted to prayer for guidance, and then, having received no answer, turned to his dreams, to his advisers, and to prophets successively. In all these he failed. In his desperation, he himself sought out a medium, a woman at Endor. Through her he sought contact with the departed spirit of Samuel, whom the medium called "a god coming up out of the earth," to whom Saul "bowed with his face to the ground, and did obeisance." The message he received through the medium was a prophecy of his own failure as king because the Lord had "torn the kingdom out of . . . [his] hand" and given it to David. Filled with fear at the words of Samuel, Saul lost his strength from not having eaten for a day and a night. Later, having been wounded in battle, and facing capture by the enemy, he killed himself by falling upon his sword (I Sam. 31:4).

This is one of the most complete psychosocial histories of an emotionally disturbed religious leader to be found in Judeo-Christian Scriptures. It demonstrates how idolatry of the dead and a resort to magic and superstition both converged in the disabling illness and final suicide of a religious leader. Anton Boisen repeatedly said that acute emotional illnesses are a reaction to a gross sense of personal failure. The story of Saul is replete with an increasing pattern of failure. The male religious leader is likely to stay well or get sick emotionally in terms of his vocational success or failure. This is amply verified in the two cases in the previous chapter. A religious leader comes more nearly to staking his or her whole life on the success or failure of the day's work.

In this respect, *idolatry of one's role* is the most common form of sick religion among religious leaders. The resort to magic and superstition as "means of cunning" to maintain and secure one's "position" or "role" as a religious leader is the next most prevalent expression of the pathology of religious leadership.

IDEALIZATION AND OMNICOMPETENCE

This one hypothesis as to the role of pathology in the religious vocation can be stated: the investment of one's total destiny in one's power to perform a given "job" as a religious leader results in fictitious goals for life that produce a pathological religion. In turn, these fictitious goals blend with the person's illusion of omnipotence and denial of human limitations. A secondary reaction is that, moving upon the fictitious goal of one's own omnicompetence, the religion of the sick religious leader tends to deteriorate into magic, cleverness, and manipulation.

An example of this kind of pathological religious leadership is that of a case entitled "The Case of Father M.," by Herbert Holt, M.D. The case is extensively presented and will be summarized here. (Herbert Holt, "The Case of Father M.: A Segment of an Existential Analysis," *Journal of Existentialism,* Vol. VI, No. 24, 1966, pp. 366–395.)

Father M. is a Catholic priest studying in a secular university in order to achieve double competency in both the priesthood and a secular profession as well.

His presenting symptoms included a plan to dismiss all incompetent priests and to reorganize the whole Catholic priesthood. He had a labyrinthine plan for doing this. He agreed to seek psychiatric help in order to enlist the psychiatrist in his plans for reorganizing the priesthood. He was a domineering man, cynical, superior, a know-it-all who felt that humility, though theoretically a Christian virtue, would deny a man of his talent his rightful leadership role. He felt that people existed in order to fulfill his demands. Those who would make him promises and fail to keep them were hypocrites deserving of his hatred. As Dr. Holt says, his view of himself and his world "was the only reality he accepted, and he reinforced this acceptance by believing what he heard himself saying."

The history and background. Father M. was one of a large family of children. His earliest memories were of habits of crying, soiling himself, and thinking of himself as a "great pig" and that his body was an alien "thing" to him. He had a sense of inner worthlessness occasioned by much sexual preoccupation. He had homosexual episodes with his older brothers. He defied his mother because he felt she neglected him and did not help him solve his great feelings of loneliness.

Father M.'s religious interests began when he turned into puberty. He refused to take up swimming because it was "charged with sexuality" for him. He was frightened by aggressive girls. His sexuality went to autoerotism, except for one instance when he unsuccessfully sought to seduce a girl. As a result, he was awakened to new religious commitment at a church retreat. He committed himself totally to his mother and made a habit of accompanying her each day to early Mass. Religion also became a weapon for controlling the rest of the family when they sought to assert themselves against him.

His "overbearing and inconsiderate manner was the cloak in adulthood for an overpowering inner sense of unworthiness developed in childhood." In an autobiographical note, Father M. says: "I suppose if we named the central problem we would call it *my* inhumanity. It's that I think that I should be perfect; it's the guilt from not being so that punishes me when I fail. It is that which inhibits my understanding of a poem or a picture; I don't know what is going on—what emotions are being expressed—because what is expressed is foreign to my vocabulary. Although I think I should respond, I can't because the poem elicits no real feeling. That feeling was denied long since.

"That inhumanity comes from my father. Father was authority. In my desire to please my father, to get his love, I had to please authority, and to please authority, I imitated it. So I have imitated it until it has become fairly habitual with me. I am probably as much like my father as he could make me.

"If I am to get free from this inhumanity, this superman humanity, I've got to throw off this need for authority and its approval, and free myself from the straitjacket it imposes.

"I thought for a while that I might go into the Army, without finishing school, in order to break away from my parents. But that would only put me under the rule of a greater authority, and the temptation to get approval from it would probably be too great. Instead of trying to become one of the men, I would alienate myself from them in trying to get above them."

This is one side of the religious haughtiness of Father M. However, a written message to Dr. Holt from the mother of the patient throws new light on the dynamics of his commitment to the priesthood. She wrote:

"I was very unhappy with my husband when I became pregnant with my boy. He spent very little time with me and the children, and I was very lonely. One day when my son was twelve years of age we all started to talk about what the children would become. I knew that my tender-hearted son could not cope with life outside, and so I told him that I wanted him to be a priest, but my son at that time wanted to become an architect, which would mean eight years of study. When he said so, his father flew into a rage and started to beat him in front of us all, hitting him with his fists all over his head and body, knocking out one tooth so that he bled from his mouth. We stepped between them to avoid further injury. My husband went to his bedroom, packed a bag, and said, 'I'm leaving.' He started to leave, but my son, bleeding from his mouth, said, 'Please, Daddy, come back. Don't leave. I'll be a good boy. I'll leave and go to school.' He left next day, a pretty dejected fellow."

The pathology of religious leadership in Father M. is a poignant story of a desperate appeal for a "greater than

he" who could be a "Saviour he had not found in the
Church or his family." He projected his denied wish, not
upon God, but on his own self-image. This grew more
and more unrealistic in its idealization and omnicompetence. He idealized his own self-image on the positive side
of his conscious *Eigenwelt*. However, his sadness over his
mother's neglect of him and his unrepeatable woe over
his father's punishment of him held him in bondage to
his loneliness and rejection.

The intensely absent reality in the story of Father M.
is that of any dialogical relationship to God himself. He
experiences religion as a "thing" that he touches only by
proxy. Forms of religion are the tools of his pathetic
fantasies of power, but they are not "means of grace"
whereby his self-rejection of himself as a "great pig" is
nullified and replaced by an acceptance of an enjoyment
of his inner life and personal space.

THE POWER ORIENTATION OF RELIGIOUS LEADERS

Whereas the refusal to accept his humanity lay close to
the heart of Father M.'s grandiosity, the honest and un-
abashed search for power for its own sake results differently. It evolves into a more sociopathic personality
disorder.

This is seen in embryo in an intensive, in-depth study
of seventeen theological students by Richard Hester. He
found that five of the students felt their pastoral authority helped them to overcome "a sense of personal impo-
tence" and to secure "personal power they would not have
otherwise." Two others understood pastoral leadership
and authority as a means of securing power over others.

Hester says that there is another, healthier alternative, and that is a *functional* rather than a *power* implementation of the leadership authority of the pastor. Six of his subjects were found to be implementing their authority as a religious leader in order to serve others rather than serve their own power needs. These students varied in their maturity within this grouping, however. One of them was absorbed in pressing technology to serve mankind by giving himself to amateur radio announcing and mastering electronic devices for "the common good." Three of these students took an immanent, humanistic view of the work of God and saw themselves "meeting human needs." Only two of these students showed a theocentric focus of their identity as a pastor. The remaining six of the group of seventeen students were suffering severe anxiety because underlying conflicts with parents, the need to be perfect, and ambivalence about being an adult kept them from a wholehearted participation in or a frank disavowal of the authority usually vested in a religious leader.

The sociopathic power orientation of the religious leader does not of itself take the leader into a hospital. Rather, his inner dividedness takes form in the groups he seeks to lead. Almost instinctively, and certainly by reason of his inconsistent and/or ambivalent parental upbringing, this person divides and conquers the groups he leads. Without forethought or plan, he effects transactions that give him a ringside seat while others fight. Occasionally this boomerangs. Those whom he has set over against each other join forces against him with the deadly purpose of hanging him from the nearest, highest yardarm or tree! Ordinarily, however, the leadership of this person only causes one minor conflict after another in the lives of those whom he purports to lead. He is known for the number of people who *leave* his church, school, or movement. Resignation is one sure way out from under the leadership of a person who divides and conquers those whom he leads. Pope John XXIII presented the antithesis of this kind of leadership as he said:

> May everyone of us be able to say: I have not dug furrows for division and distrust, I have not darkened immortal souls with suspicion or fear; I have been frank, loyal and trustful; I have looked those who do not share my ideals straight in the eye and treated them with brotherly affection in order not to impede God's great purpose. (John P. Donnelly, ed., *Prayers and Devotions from Pope John XXIII*, p. 31; Grossett & Dunlap, Inc., 1967.)

The work of Richard Hester plainly indicates that the sociopathic *use* of the place of religious leadership can be identified, detected, and confronted for what it is in the process of theological education. Also, John M. MacDonald suggests ways for quickly identifying the sociopathic personality. Prompt ways are needed in order to confront the sociopathic religious leader *before* he gains access to the forms of religion for the sake of the power and authority vested in them by the religious community.

MacDonald suggests that the deliberate use of vague and extensive language to answer questions is one evidence of the sociopath: he protects his real position with an abundance of vague words. Yet, the sociopathic person persuades himself that he is a very truthful person because he answers other people's questions very literally.

For example, when asked if he has ever applied to a theological seminary before, he will answer with a no. What he means, he convinces himself, is that he has never applied to *this* seminary before. In fact, he has applied to three and been rejected by all three. Therefore, three or four questions, not one, must be asked: (1) Has he ever applied to this seminary before? (2) Has he ever applied to any other seminary anywhere else? (3) Which seminary accepted him? (4) Which seminary rejected him and why?

MacDonald says that the psychopathic (or sociopathic) person often demonstrates both paranoid and depressive reactions, especially when caught in misdemeanors or frustrated in his or her global sense of power. The sociopath, says MacDonald, undetected and allowed to go unhindered, may be found in places of high rank. (John M. MacDonald, "The Prompt Diagnosis of the Psychopathic Personality," Supplement to the *American Journal of Psychiatry*, Vol. 122, No. 12, June, 1966, pp. 45–50.) Obviously, the best strategy in dealing with the sociopathic person is early detection and elimination from places of religious leadership.

THE PATHOLOGY OF RELIGIOUS LEADERSHIP AS SEEN IN BREAKS WITH REALITY

Among the schizophrenic group of mental patients are found persons whose illness is focused upon a kind of religious perception that has only minimal contact with reality. The religious consciousness of these patients has been studied by Howe, Boisen, and Rokeach at different times and in different places over the last half century.

Farr and Howe

In the late twenties and early thirties, Clifford Farr, M.D., and the Reverend Reul Howe made a study of the influence of religious ideas on the psychoses. (Clifford B. Farr and Reuel Howe, "The Influence of Religious Ideas on the Etiology, Symptomatology, and Prognosis of the Psychoses," *The American Journal of Psychiatry*, Vol. II, 1933, pp. 845–865.) They noted the combined effect of both social and religious isolation, a marked factor in leadership of any kind, now spoken of as "executive loneliness." Farr and Howe extended their study to five hundred consecutive cases, 342 females and 158 males. Fourteen percent, or sixty-eight cases, "were found with definite religious content."

From the point of view of the pathology of religious leadership, several factors may be extrapolated from their work: First, the emotional breakdowns of religious leaders who are doing their work because of a desire to fulfill other people's wishes that they be religious workers rather than because of their own personal choice to do so. The following case excerpt is illustrative:

> Case 11130, female, 34, Church of the Brethren. Diagnosis: manic-depressive psychosis, mixed. The patient was brought up in a strongly religious environment to be a missionary, but she was not a very enthusiastic one. She also studied nursing. In the mission field she was considered a very efficient worker, but broke down. There had been a conflict between her own sense of inadequacy and lack of inclination for the work and the unconscious pressure of the family and the religious denomination. In her psychosis there were pronounced mood swings. (*Ibid.*, p. 858.)

A second case illustrates an interpretation of emotional illness as a call to religious leadership in its own right. A woman "claims that after seeing the Lord Jesus, she was saved, and that God sent her to the hospital to save others because she had been restrained too much in the past." (*Ibid.*, p. 861.) As another patient, in interpreting her childlike behavior, told me, "I was never permitted to be a child when I was a child and now I am catching up when I can."

Farr and Howe concluded their study with a discussion by Clarence B. Farrar, who used the threefold classification of William Osler to distinguish mental patients' religious concerns. Osler said that the doctrine of immortality and other religious beliefs were accepted differently by men. One group he named the "Laodiceans," a majority, who accept a belief but their lives are uninfluenced by it. Another and smaller group he named the "Gallionians," after Gallio, "who cared for none of these things." The third group, and the smallest one, are the "Theresans," who, like St. Theresa, the Carmelite nun, are deeply religious folk "for whom the life of the spirit is the only real life." (*Ibid.*, p. 863; see also Harvey Cushing, *The Life of Sir William Osler*, pp. 597–598, 639–641; Oxford University Press, Inc., 1940.) Among the mentally ill, as in the general population, there are very few persons for whom the life of the spirit is the only real life.

Anton T. Boisen

However, Anton Boisen would contend that there *are* a few persons who feel this way and that their sense of commitment should be taken seriously, even though they seem "crazy" to the Laodiceans!

Boisen calls attention to the process whereby a "deviating set of religious beliefs are translated into social organization." He says that such religious leaders as George Fox (1624–1691), the English founder of the Society of Friends, or Quakers, manifested many of the behaviors of mental patients today:

> Inventors, poets, and others who do creative work have such experiences frequently. Among men of religious genius they are of crucial importance. They figure in what is called "inspiration" or "revelation." Most religious movements are based upon faith in the divine authority of some such experiences. . . . Great religious leaders . . . have had their inspirations, their revelations, their messages from the Lord. But so also do many mental patients. They too hear God talking to them and believe that they have been given a prophetic mission. (Anton T. Boisen, "The Development and Validation of Religious Faith," *Psychiatry: Journal for the Study of Interpersonal Processes,* Vol. 14, No. 4, Nov., 1951, p. 455.)

Boisen then sets himself to the task of distinguishing a true prophet from a false, "and how a deviating set of beliefs are organized and tested," thus bringing about a social reform and a new social organization. One criterion he uses is the *historical continuity* of a leader like Fox with previous, tested, and approved prophets like Calvin. Continuity is *one* of the "operations of common sense." Another criterion is consistency of stabilized social effectiveness in communicating the beliefs to others. This consistency is based upon a kind of humility about the contradictions and complexities that still remain. In other words, there is an openness and teachability in the true prophet that does not appear in the paranoid, grandiose, and persecutory attitudes of some mentally sick religious leaders. Such patients are not acutely disturbed, says Boisen, but are drifting and surrendering to self-concealment and deception.

A genuine consistency in the true prophet prompts him to test his insights and revelations "by some stream of tradition," by social criticism and acceptance, and by the social consequences they produce. Through this social process, new ideas are assimilated into social organizations.

In an extensive case history of a black patient named Mickle, Boisen discusses the concept of the patient as a religious leader in the light of his psychopathology. He concludes by saying that the "signals" or voices that Mickle got from God needed to be taken seriously as stirrings of a religious concern.

> The medieval mystics had to learn the lesson that some of the ideas which came surging into their minds could hardly come from God. They assumed that they must have come from the devil. Perhaps we of today need to learn the converse lesson, that all auditory hallucinations do not necessarily come from the devil but may represent the operations of the creative mind. (Anton T. Boisen, "Inspiration in the Light of Psychopathology," *Pastoral Psychology,* Oct., 1960, pp. 10–18.)

Anton Boisen was my teacher. I have often heard him say that it takes more than one generation to judge whether a religious leader is crazy or not, that the mentally sick person may be in an acute fever of religious concern as he finds his real direction in life and place in the world, and that a genuine religious leader can be separated from the counterfeit by his humility or openness to instruction from others.

Søren Kierkegaard

However, these wise sayings are not complete, and Boisen would be the first to say that he, too, prophesies in part. An even more complete approach to distinguishing between fantasy and reality is made by Søren Kierkegaard in his book-length case study of a Danish religious leader named Adolph Peter Adler. (Søren Kierkegaard, *On Authority and Revelation,* tr. by Walter Lowrie; Princeton University Press, 1955.)

In 1843 Adler published his *Sermons.* He said that although he had been a teacher in the State Church prior to this, the Spirit of God "commanded him to burn everything he had formerly written." He felt called by a revelation, appealed to this revelation, and began to exert authority and leadership "in the strength of the fact that he was called by a revelation." This revelation came to Adler at the age of twenty-two. As a result of Adler's "revelations," Bishop Mynster suspended him as a clergyman on the grounds that his mind was deranged, and in another year deposed him. He was given a small pension, which gave him the leisure to continue to write books against the church. He saw himself as a John the Baptist. In an interview with Adler, Kierkegaard said to him that he could discover no new revelation in Adler's work. Then Adler told him that the book had to be read aloud in a whistling voice before its meaning would be open to him.

Kierkegaard's discussion of Adler's situation takes into account the cultural "characterlessness" of the times against which Adler was reacting. Kierkegaard says that "when an age becomes characterless it is possible that one or another individual may show symptoms of wishing to be extraordinary." (Kierkegaard, *On Authority and Revelation*, p. 33.) However, Kierkegaard questions Adler's authenticity at two points. First, Adler expected the "established order" to join forces with him to let him be extraordinary, unusual, and different. (*Ibid.*) At the same time, the pathology of Adler rested not in the source of his authority in God but in his shift of his concept of his own purpose and calling in life. He made himself "presumptuously into a genius, whereas God called him to be an apostle." (*Ibid.*, p. 24.) "The genius is what he is by reason of himself, i.e., by what he is in himself; an apostle is what he is by reason of divine authority." (*Ibid.*, p. 105.) And, what makes this difference between the ordinary individual and the special individual is *the starting point*. (*Ibid.*, p. 36.) Then Kierkegaard describes in a short space of words the nature of the true as over against the false religious leader:

> Thus it is with the true *extraordinarius:* he is the most carefree man in comparison with the world's temporal anxiety as to whether what he has to proclaim will be triumphant in the world; on the other hand, he is as much in anguish as a poor sinner with a contrite heart whenever he thinks of his responsibility, whether in any way he might be mistaken; yea for him it is as though his breathing were obstructed, so heavily weighs the weight of his responsibility upon him. (*Ibid.*, p. 39.)

Finally, Kierkegaard epitomizes the ambiguity of the religious leader who veers away from reality as it is represented in the established order of Christendom, which is essentially pagan:

> Just then when he had come nearer to being a Christian than ever before during all the time he was a Christian, just then was he deposed. . . . As a pagan he became a Christian priest, and . . . when he had undeniably come somewhat nearer to being a Christian he was deposed.

Milton Rokeach

One of the most detailed studies of the pathology of religious leadership is by Rokeach. (Milton Rokeach, *The Three Christs of Ypsilanti: A Psychological Study;* Alfred A. Knopf, Inc., 1964.) Over a period from July 1, 1959, to August 15, 1961, Rokeach met with three male patients who considered themselves to be Christ. These patients were in real life named Clyde, Leon, and Joseph. They were patients at Ypsilanti State Hospital, near Ann Arbor, Michigan. At the time of the study, the hospital had 4,100 patients, 5 staff psychiatrists, and 20 resident psychiatrists. Clyde was close to seventy years of age, Joseph was about sixty, and Leon was in his late thirties. Joseph and Clyde had been in the hospital nearly twenty years and Leon had been there five years.

Each of these patients had a chronic paranoid-schizophrenic diagnosis, and this included the exalted conception of himself as the Christ and a steady resistance to entry into this delusional system to change it. Rokeach and members of the staff moved the patients into the same living quarters and developed a similar daily routine for all of them. A regular confrontation-type group session was conducted each week by Rokeach. The confrontation left Clyde and Joseph, the two older men, essentially unchanged. Leon's story changed slowly but surely as he groped with the riddle of his own identity. The most significant summary statement of Rokeach says that there was "a basic difference in the grandiose delusions of Clyde and Joseph on the one hand and Leon on the other." (*Ibid.*, p. 326.) This basic difference provided a working hypothesis for understanding and helping persons suffering from less chronic pathologies of religious vocation. Clyde and Joseph expressed the dominant theme of both vocational and sexual *"shame* over feelings of *incompetence* as a male."* These are not guilt-ridden Christs, they are more preoccupied with being great than good. And the religious element is not especially prominent. These are the end result of the "power-orientation" religious leaders. They are plagued by the fear of incompetence, inadequacy, and fears of weakness *as men.* To accept their humanity would be to give in to these fears. As Rokeach says of Clyde and Joseph:

> Clyde is Christ because he needs to be "the biggest one." He is preoccupied with the carloads of money, land and women he owns. And Joseph is God, Christ and the Holy Ghost because these are the biggest personages one can be. If there were a super-God, Joseph would have been super-God. (*Ibid.*, p. 327.)

On the other hand, Leon's dominant theme is not shame over "incompetence but *guilt* about forbidden sexual and aggressive impulses. He is forever tormented with inadmissible impulses. . . . Leon is a guilt-ridden Christ who strives to be good rather than great; he is suffering not so much from a delusion of greatness as from a delusion of goodness." (*Ibid.*, p. 327.) Rokeach documents this conclusion from a minute study of each patient's developmental history. Here again the admission of human guilt would be as threatening to Leon as the admission of human weakness and lack of power would be to Clyde and Joseph.

In all three instances, however, the theological problem of salvation is that of a willingness to be a participant in the incarnation as well as an inheritor of its symbols in identification as the Christ. The real Christ was *willing* to accept his human limitations and temptations. These sick "Christs" were not. This is the issue in the development of adequate religious leaders. Can we enable them toward what Stephen Neill calls a "genuinely human existence"? Can they be encouraged early to know their real strengths and accept their real limitations? Can they very early experience forgiveness and be able to enjoy their human strengths of love and aggression rather than languish in guilt? If so, they themselves need leaders who enjoy a sense of adequacy, can provide a genuine permission to them to exercise their powers, and can give them protection as they learn to do so. For, as the pastoral epistle puts it, "God did not give us a spirit of timidity, but a spirit of power and love and self-control" (II Tim. 1:7).

"DITCHING" OF RESPONSIBILITY AND THE PATHOLOGY OF RELIGIOUS LEADERSHIP

The "three Christs" represent a psychotic break with reality as a way of handling their unbearable feelings of inadequacy and burdens of guilt. They took this route rather than a sociopathic *use* of religious leadership as a means of power and gratification. However, in conclusion, the neurotic-depressive route is taken by a larger number of people in religious work, it seems to me. In these instances, the feelings of incompetence and/or guilt are displaced into some kind of otherwise meaningless "behaviors." These acts, in turn, jettison responsibility and "get the person out" of responsibilities that they can neither carry out with effectiveness nor admit with honor that they cannot or do not want to do. A list of such "odd behaviors" is as follows: a graduate student of divinity is caught making obscene telephone calls to women; just prior to his first pastorate, a minister is caught exhibiting himself sexually to young girls; a middle-aged pastor "gets out" of an executive position by taking certain money for his own use; a leading layman in a denomination gets caught embezzling funds; etc. These symptoms are what I have named "ditching" symptoms. In a depressed, self-deprecating crisis, the person ditches his high-altitude pilot's position of leadership. The behavior both gets him out of his seat of responsibility and punishes him publicly for doing so.

This handling of leadership in a pathological way is not restricted to religious leaders. Political figures have the same problem, as was evident in the case of the assistant to President Johnson who was caught in an episode of homosexual behavior.

The economy of such "ditching" symptoms is to preserve the total life of the person from literal suicide by accomplishing a professional suicide instead. It is better for a part—the prestige—of the person to be destroyed than for the whole life to end. On the other hand, a more creative alternative would be for the person to examine with psychotherapeutic assistance some of his needs for "proving his competence" and to discover more direct, courageous, and verbal ways of getting out of unrealistic and unbearable stress with honor and dignity.

With this objective, a pastor can do much to be an instrument of God's grace in enabling men and women toward a more "reasonable service" to God by anticipating crises in people's lives when they are under inordinate stress of positions of power and public service. He should be able occasionally to get to people *before* they hit the panic button and jettison their responsibilities.

In Summary

This chapter has dealt with the ways in which religious leadership is a focus for the pathology of religion. Attention has been given to the ways in which idealization and omnicompetence needs distort the religious calling. The power orientation of the sociopathic religious leader has been identified in both its inception and its floration. The schizophrenic unreality of the searches for ultimate competence and ultimate goodness in human form was thoroughly discussed. The final discussion was of the flight from responsibility in the "ditching" symptoms of "acting out" kinds of infantile behavior in religious leaders.

Chapter 8

RELIGIOUS FACTORS
IN MENTAL ILLNESS

In 1955 I published a book entitled *Religious Factors in Mental Illness* (Association Press, 1955). This subject needs revisiting. The issues of life and death, hope and hopelessness, meaning and meaninglessness involved in mental illness remain the same. The battleground on which these issues are fought out, however, is very different. The armaments for waging the battle have changed radically. The aftermath of the Korean War found mentally ill persons adjusting to the renewed demands of competition in the civilian pursuits of life. The quest for affluence had begun to gather momentum in America but was not at its peak speed. The psychotropic drugs had begun to take hold but had not changed the face of the hospital care of the mentally ill nor made the ambulatory treatment of the mentally ill as possible as is apparent on every hand today. The religious ideation of mental patients described in my book published in 1955 is much more obscure to the ear of the therapist today. The pastor and the chaplain must have much better ears for it since patients are "quieted" or "elevated" chemically, even by their general physicians. Furthermore, the rapid advances in milieu and community therapy, pointing toward the outpatient treatment of the mentally ill in a variety of highly imaginative residential settings, have added to the importance of the community as a healing factor, underscored so heavily in the 1955 version of my book *Religious Factors in Mental Illness*.

In 1967 I published a monograph in the *Internationales Jahrbuch für Religionssoziologie* in West Germany. In this monograph, I sought to bring up to that date some of the salient changes in the understanding of the psychopathology of religion.

The substance of the 1955 book and the 1967 monograph is still effectively valid. Persons of the stature of Anton Boisen and colleagues of mine who have been lifelong students of the relation between religion and psychiatry have not encouraged a revision of the book. They suggest that it stand as it is. There has been no suggestion of revision of the monograph. The purpose of this chapter, then, is this: to write a sequel to the book and the monograph. I will bring out emphases of the intervening years that update my understanding of the religious factors in mental illness and summarize the data of this book accordingly.

Both popular folklore and scientific attempts at empirical analysis have focused attention upon the role of religion in mental illness. This book presents some of the empirical data that have been collected on this subject. These data suggest some hypotheses as to the function of religion in mental disorders, both as a causative and a curative factor. Such a study has been intended to offset some of the superstitious accretions that hasten to the mind about the relation of religion and mental illness.

RELIGION AS A FACTOR

However, problems of methodology call for a clear summary of the meaning of the thought of religion as *a factor* in life. Kurt Lewin has clarified the methodological difficulties involved in the factorial approach to any subject. The contemporary scientist is debtor both to Aristotle's philosophy and to Galileo's scientific philosophy. The Aristotelian approach to the study of phenomena isolates, describes, and categorizes various factors about the phenomena. This classification of religion as a "factor" among many "factors" in the phenomenon of mental illness is in the Aristotelian tradition of categorizing and describing. From this vantage point, this discussion of religious factors in mental illness assumes that there are other factors in mental illness than religion. We cannot reduce mental illness to one phenomenon and to one cause, although popular antagonism to religion tends to do this. Religion is only one factor in mental illness.

The Galilean approach to science, however, emphasizes the totality of things. The holistic thinker redirects attention to the dangers of overclassification. From this point of view, religion would be seen as implicit in all other factors as well as a neatly categorized factor in and of itself. The research person's scientific methodology itself has elements of reverence and awe that are compatible with the total religious mood toward life. We can "bracket out" religious factors in mental illness.

The bracketing, however, is for purposes of investigation and study only, to be reintegrated later. It cannot obscure the reality of religion as an implicit if not explicit dimension of all human existence. These two perspectives—the Aristotelian and the Galilean—must be held in focus, therefore, in the study of religious factors in mental illness. (Kurt Lewin, *A Dynamic Theory of Personality,* pp. 1–42; McGraw-Hill Book Company, Inc., 1935.)

With this kind of perspective, then, the following factors have been identified by a variety of research persons as *religious* factors in mental illness. The reader will recall that in Chapter 1 I defined a healthy faith as an expression of the total personality of an individual in his relationship to the Divine as a comprehensive and ultimate loyalty. Also, sick religion was defined as being that kind of religious belief or practice that makes itself a thing apart from the totality of life of the whole person. Religion becomes an "it," a compartmentalized thing to be "used" as a defense against life rather than lived as a way of life. This is what makes of it a "factor" in the Aristotelian sense.

RELIGIOUS AFFILIATION AND MENTAL ILLNESS

Lenski defines "the religious factor" in terms of devotionalism and doctrinal orthodoxy in the affiliation of a person with a communal faith group. (Gerhard Lenski, *The Religious Factor,* pp. 23–24; Doubleday & Company, Inc., 1961.) One asks if there is any correlation between religious affiliation and mental illness. E. Gartly Jaco studied residents of Texas who were diagnosed as being psychotic according to the classification system of the American Psychiatric Association. The patients studied were those who sought psychiatric treatment for the first time in their lives during 1951 and 1952. The following data were recorded by Jaco concerning the religious affiliation of these patients (E. Gartly Jaco, *The Social Epidemiology of Mental Disorders,* p. 193; Russell Sage Foundation, 1960):

| | PSYCHOTIC GROUP | | TOTAL TEXAS |
	Number of Cases	Percent	POPULATION Percent
Religious Affiliation			
Protestant	7,167	79.4	70.8
Roman Catholic	1,429	15.8	28.2
Hebrew	72	0.8	1.0
Other	11	0.1	0.0
None	348	3.9	0.0
Total	9,027	100.0	100.0[b]

[b] These estimates of religious affiliation are based on recent censuses of the Texas and National Council of Churches. However, these censuses represent only 54.6 percent of the Texas population.

On the basis of these data, one could speculate as to whether mental illness does not increase as the loss of a sense of an intact, cohesive religious group increases. The group itself can compartmentalize and distort religion. Fallding and others have demonstrated conclusively that alcoholism, one form of emotional disorder, increases as alcohol consumption becomes either an assuagement or a retaliation for the loss of acceptance by and secure participation in a communal group. Harold Fallding,

"The Source and Burden of Civilization Illustrated in the Use of Alcoholism," *The Quarterly Journal of Studies on Alcohol,* Vol. XXV, No. 4, Dec., 1964, pp. 714–724.)

ISOLATION AND MENTAL ILLNESS

The religious factor in life may be further defined in terms of the paradoxical tension existing between the need to be an individual and the need for community. (Wayne E. Oates, *Religious Dimensions of Personality,* pp. 41–46; Association Press, 1957.) This point of view is most apparent in the contribution of Anton Boisen to the understanding of religious factors in mental illness. Briefly stated, his point of view is that the loss of fellowship with the community "whose approval one considers most worthwhile" creates a crisis of sin and salvation for an individual. He may meet this crisis in a constructive or a destructive way. In both instances, he may become emotionally ill. Mental illness is like a fever in the body: it is nature's attempt to heal the total being of the person. He said that some illnesses are malignant in that the person uses concealment and defense, pride, and self-justification as a way of dealing with the threat to his life. Other mental illnesses are benign in that they are characterized by *concern*. The self-searching and concern takes on a religious character as the person seeks to define his place and vocation in life. This kind of mental illness Boisen defined as a search for salvation. To Boisen, this search is the religious factor in mental illness. The issue at stake in the mental patient's redemption is his responsibly living as an individual in a community of faith. The illness is characterized by isolation. Healing is made possible by a discovery and acceptance of a community. (Anton Boisen, *The Exploration of the Inner World;* Harper & Row, Publishers, Inc., 1952.)

This particular aspect of the religious factor in mental illness was identified by Sigmund Freud. He contrasted the obsessional neurosis with religious ritual. He defined an obsessional neurosis as a "private religion" in that the obsession is compulsive, ritualistic, and methodical. Furthermore, the obsession seeks to communicate the guilt at the same time it assuages it. However, Freud distinguished the obsessional practice from the religious practice. (Sigmund Freud, "Obsessive Acts and Religious Practices," *Collected Papers,* Vol. II, 2d ed., pp. 25–35; Hogarth Press, 1942.) Religious practice is communal in character. The neurotic is isolated and individualistic. From this hypothesis Freud stated his conception by locating the universal sense of guilt in the murder of the father of the primal horde by the younger aspirants for his place. (Sigmund Freud, "Totem and Taboo," *The Basic Writings of Sigmund Freud,* tr. by A. A. Brill, pp. 807–930; Modern Library, 1938.) Only in this highly speculative way does the father of modern psychoanalysis come to terms with the communal aspect of religion in illness and health.

IDOLATRY AS A RELIGIOUS FACTOR IN MENTAL ILLNESS

We have seen in Chapter 2 that idolatry is a potent religious factor in mental illness. Here religion is sick at its heart. The quest for acceptance may be directed toward a constricted and limited community of faith. The most conspicuous kind of growth-limiting community is the family itself. Mental illness is related to isolation and the need for community. But, on the other hand, the community itself may be limited and constricted. Its demand for allegiance may retard, reverse, or prevent altogether the normal growth of the personality of an individual member. The person capitulates to the demands of the family or communal group. He renounces the demands of his own growth. Thereby, he becomes sick.

The author studied religious groups in eastern Kentucky in the United States in relation to members of the groups who were admitted to state mental hospitals. Two major findings were evident. First, some patients became ill when they remained in the confines of a very restricted religious group made up of one, two, or three families who were interrelated to each other by marriage and the economic pursuit of farming. These ingroups were what is known in Kentucky and other American frontier states as "clans." Within these groups, a young person or a person in early or middle adulthood would tend to become sick from the accumulation of unfulfilled developmental tasks. They had omitted having close friends their own age, learning to be independent of the family structure, having the right to choose their own mate in a culture where this is the norm, and becoming economically and socially independent of their parental home. In the second place, other persons would become sick when they attempted but failed in their attempts to leave the familial religious group and become a member of another group. Thus they were isolated and caught in a religious "no-man's-land" of loneliness and misunderstanding. (Oates, *Religious Factors in Mental Illness,* p. 92.)

In both these instances, the religious factor in the illness was a bondage to the idolatry of the small, restricted, communal unit. In the eastern Kentucky hospital study, seventeen out of sixty-eight cases of psychotic disorder revealed a long-term conflict between the individual and his family that ran along religious lines. (*Ibid.*, p. 78.) The religious loyalty of the family housed the parental domination and control of the child. Religion was used as a means of maintaining control of the child. A comparative study of mission volunteers done later, however, revealed that religion was the main means of rebellion and autonomy used by these young persons. When the young person found support and protection from isolation in a new religious group, he did not become mentally sick in any psychotic sense wherein he broke away from reality. Rather, he became something of a religious "rebel," delinquent against his parents. He effected his autonomy of his parents through the use of religion. Many times after the rebellion was effected the religion was discarded.

These ideas suggest a working hypothesis concerning the role of religion in mental illness and health. The religious institution is a secondary institution to the home. Next to the home, it has, in time, first access to the developing child. Children who go to church do so before they go to kindergarten, public school, etc. Furthermore, the church has access to the parents at the same time, as well as to the grandparents or great-grandparents. The cycle of the generations is or may be represented at every age level and at every generation level in the church. In other words, the church has access to the whole family constellation. Therefore, the church, depending upon the leadership's understanding of familial and religious factors in mental illness, is in a remarkably strategic position to change unhealthy patterns of emotional development. Without insight and understanding on the part of the religious leadership, however, the church may contribute to unhealthy patterns of emotional development in children. Religion may become the means of domineering and even incestuous distortion of the child's life by parents who demand idolatry of their children.

From a prophylactic point of view, one could state this hypothesis of the function of religion in man's struggle for emotional stability in the following way. In the growing person, religion and its institutions encourage the tender emotions of caring for little children. As has been said several times in this book, religion lowers the importance of the earthly family of the adolescent, gives the adolescent a safe mooring of ethical values for his hostilities and sensuality, and enables him to form comprehensive loyalties to the larger family of mankind. In this larger family, the smaller idolatries of life are challenged by prophetic religion. The comprehensive, ultimate loyalties and concerns of life are made clear and relevant to the individual. Such religion leads to health. Anything less than this leads to constriction of growth and emotional disorder. Furthermore, as was seen in Chapter 3, the issue of idolatrous religion is a practice of magic and superstition as religion.

Gordon Allport, professor of psychology at Harvard University, describes, as was seen earlier, the mature religious sentiment as having a comprehensive character. Communism, for example, has a certain religious quality, but its sentiment is not comprehensive and does not include all of that which is permanent in life. Allport agrees with Whitehead, who said that religion deals comprehensively with "what is permanent in the nature of things." (Alfred North Whitehead, *Religion in the Making*, p. 16; The Macmillan Company, 1926.) Wholehearted zeal for a cause does act like a religious sentiment, but it has a pseudoreligious cast. Allport says that even from a psychological point of view such causes and secular interests "fall short of the range that characterizes a mature religious sentiment which seems never satisfied unless it is dealing with matters central to all existence." (Gordon Allport, *The Individual and His Religion*, p. 69.) From this vantage point, then, a person is immature and may become emotionally off-center and "eccentric," if not sick, when he commits himself to that which is partial and limited as an ultimate loyalty of his life. Hence Allport's definition of religion as man's "ultimate attempt to enlarge and complete his own personality by finding the supreme context in which he rightly belongs." (*Ibid.*, p. 78.)

Carl Jung developed his concept of the "complex" with this working hypothesis of the comprehensiveness of the context in which the individual rightly belongs. He defined a "complex" as "active contents of the unconscious [which] . . . have been split off from consciousness and lead a separate existence in the unconscious, being at all times ready to hinder or reinforce the conscious intentions." (Carl G. Jung, *The Integration of the Personality*, pp. 156–157; London: Routledge and Kegan Paul, Ltd., 1945.) Plato poetically described this domination of the personality by the partial, restricted, and temporary values of life as "the rising up of a part of the soul against the whole." The vital function of psychol-

ogy and psychiatry today, therefore, is to challenge the
petty idolatries of hearthstone gods, family fortunes, and
cultural and racial mythologies that turn an individual
and a culture away from health into emotional disorder
and illness. In this sense, the study of psychopathology
by theologians and pastors alike serves to purify their
teaching and practice of that which limits and constricts
the minds of their followers as surely as the primitive
practice of foot-binding of Chinese children prevented
the growth of their bodies.

As was seen in Chapter 2, the Protestant theologian
Paul Tillich has articulated this point of view in his
formulations concerning the "demonic" in human life.
He views religion as that which expresses the *ultimate*
concerns of man. These concerns transcend the proximate
and nondurable interests of man's life as an individual.
An individual may place any relative, proximate concern at the center of his existence and endow it with
ultimate significance. Then that relative and proximate
concern *possesses* him and has demonic force in his life.
Tillich calls this the "absolutizing of the relative." The
anxiety man experiences becomes pathological and can
be removed only through therapeutic means. (Tillich,
The Courage to Be, pp. 38–39.) Such pathological anxiety
is different from the ontological anxiety occasioned by the
threats of condemnation, meaninglessness, and death that
attend the existence of every individual by reason of his
being human. Here again one finds an underscoring of the
idolatrous or demonic aspect, or pathological conditions,
as one of the religious factors in mental illness.

In the care of the sick, probably no clinical situation
reveals more vividly the power of the penultimate con-

cerns of life to produce mental illness than that of the bereaved person. We focused on this experience in the discussion of idolatry. Here one is confronted with the possibility of making the deceased an object of worship. The crisis of grief calls for the kind of mature religious sentiment that both accepts the fact of death and distinguishes love for the deceased from an ultimate loyalty to the deceased. Dietrich Bonhoeffer comments on this disrelationship between "ultimate and penultimate" concerns. He recommends that the Christian pastoral approach to the bereaved situation should be one in which we adopt a "penultimate attitude." One remains silent as a sign that he "shares in the bereaved man's helplessness in the face of such a grievous event." He says that remaining silent about the ultimate confines one deliberately in the penultimate. (Dietrich Bonhoeffer, *Ethics*, p. 84; The Macmillan Company, 1955.) Grief itself is a transitional despair. Time, through a process of revelation, shows the marked difference between genuine grief over the loss of a human being and idolatry of the dead. If this transition is not made, then the person becomes mentally sick.

TRUST AND DISTRUST AS RELIGIOUS FACTORS IN MENTAL ILLNESS

One large category of mentally ill persons is characterized by major difficulties in establishing durable and trusting relationships with other persons. These patients are usually spoken of as either paranoid schizophrenic or as paranoiac, according to the nature of the organization of the grandiose, persecutory, and homoerotic dimensions of the illness. These illnesses are characterized by minimal if not nonexistent personal insight and a corresponding projection of responsibility and blame on other persons, institutions, and cosmic forces. The fabric of the being of these patients seems to have been woven from threads of distrust and basic insecurity in significant relationships. From the point of view of the positive qualities of faith that characterize religion that is healthy, this factor of trust or distrust may be defined as another religious factor in mental illness.

The psychoanalyst who has been most definitive about this factor in emotional illness and health is Erik Erikson. He describes trust as the basic emotion of human life in that its formation is the first crisis of the developing infant. As a psychopathologist he could not avoid observing that innumerable people cannot afford to be without religion and that many whose pride in not having it reminds the psychopathologist of whistling in the dark. Erikson says that the function of religion is to restore a sense of trust in the form of faith and to give tangible form to the sense of evil that religion promises to ban. Individual trust is viewed by him as a common faith, and mistrust as a common evil. Religion must derive a faith for the individual that is "transmitted to infants in the form of basic trust." Without this basic trust, life is built upon suspicion and distrust, which may become an illness. (Erikson, *Identity and the Life Cycle,* pp. 64–65.)

Rev. George Bennett conducted a two-year research project in a 1,500-patient hospital for the mentally ill. Over the two-year period, he worked with ten patients intensively—five men and five women—to study the role of religion in their lives. All these patients were predominantly suspicious, untrusting, and diagnosed as paranoid schizophrenic. None of the subjects revealed a positive relationship of love and trust between their parents; strife and tension dominated the homes of all these patients. All of the subjects were without warm and loving mothers. No positive trusting relationship existed between the patients and their fathers. Only one of the patients had an even partially satisfying marriage. None experienced emotional satisfactions in sexual relationships. Their religion was characterized by projecting the blame for their sufferings and shortcomings on God and neighbor. Each person sought systematically to interpret himself as a very good person with special identity, special gifts, and high self-esteem.

Religious life in the hospital provided some positive benefits for these patients, nevertheless, in that they were pulled out of their isolation into a corporate experience of worship. They developed better social control over unacceptable impulses, and a narrow channel of communication with the world was opened through an indirect discussion of their feelings through conversation about their prayers. The trees of the lives of these patients, Bennett says, "had poor roots and brought forth little fruit, but the trees did stand." Bennett identifies their taproot of distrust and the absence of the supporting roots of genuine trust as a religious factor in their illness. (George Bennett, "Religious Activity and the Suspicious Person," *The Journal of Pastoral Care,* Vol. XVIII, No. 3, Fall, 1964, pp. 140–147.)

In this book, the situation of the acute or chronic schizophrenic person has been best understood under the rubric of establishing a personal space, a territory that is one's own. The overbalanced need of schizophrenics to do this is symptomatic of their having "witches messages," as the tranactional analyst Robert Goulding calls them, pronounced upon them earlier in life. They were literally told not to exist, not to be, to die, to get lost, etc. Our discussion of the quest for one's own territory is made poignant by the succeeding stories of the Methodical Methodist, Father M., and the three "Christs" of Ypsilanti.

Irving M. Rosen, M.D., clinical director at the Cleveland Psychiatric Institute in Ohio, studied the role of religion in both the acutely and chronically psychotic person. He challenged the assumption that strong religious interest is necessarily to be equated with mental aberration. He continued his studies further and developed a guide to the spiritual examination of the patient's religious consciousness, history, and world view. In doing so, he did not omit examination of patients who were, so-called, unreligious. He observed that these patients usually had some sort of center to their lives, usually their mothers.

One of the most important results of applying the religious inventory to patients was the discovery of the role of reconciliation and forgiveness in the alienated and unforgiving way of life of the patient. As Rosen says, the patient "had on occasion to be encouraged to use those channels of forgiveness open to him in order to get well. With certain patients communications about anger had to be turned into the more religious terminology of reconciliation and forgiveness before their emotional lives could be tapped and opened to abreaction." (Irving M. Rosen, M.D., "Spiritual Attitude Examination in the Evaluation and Treatment of Psychiatric Patients," *The Journal of Pastoral Care,* Vol. XVII, No. 2, Summer, 1963, p. 78.) Rosen concluded that the sociopathic person, particularly, is aided in recovery through such spiritual confrontation and that the examination of spiritual attitude acted as a corrective for those who took reality either too lightly or too seriously. Forgiveness and reconciliation are absent from the life of the person who cannot trust. Erik Erikson calls this the acceptance of one's own life history and the people in it as "something that had to be" and for which there are no substitutes. (Erikson, *Identity and the Life Cycle,* p. 98.) But the religious factor in the life of the paranoid schizophrenic person rests in his intention to rewrite his own life history according to his own presuppositions whether these fit reality or not.

HOPE AND HOPELESSNESS AS A RELIGIOUS FACTOR IN MENTAL ILLNESS

The manic-depressive patient's life situation reflects another religious factor in mental illness: hope and hopelessness. Margaret Mead, professor of anthropology at Columbia University, has said that hope and hoping are the most important *cross-cultural constants* that characterize religion in all cultures. (Margaret Mead made this statement in a lecture at the 1959 Arden House conference of the Academy of Religion and Mental Health in Harriman, New York.) The religious factor in mental illness is hopelessness and the religious factor in mental health is hope. Gabriel Marcel says that hoping does not really take place until a person is visited by calamity. A person begins hoping when he is trapped. (Gabriel Marcel, *Homo Viator, Prolégomènes à une métaphysique de l'espérance;* Aubier: Editions Montaigne, 1944, quoted by Paul Pruyser in reference below.) Mental illness is such a calamity. The elaborate delusional eschatologies presented by deeply disturbed patients are desperate attempts to reconstruct a hopeful and hoping way of life.

Paul Pruyser points out that the dilemma of the mentally ill is to cope with the desperation of their life situation with hoping. Reality—seen cold-bloodedly—leads neither to despair nor hope, but to apathy. The price of sensitivity in dealing with reality with feeling is to become vulnerable to despair. Despair, however, is the paradoxical or dialectical condition of hoping. Says Pruyser, "Only against the background of 'un-hope,' or despair, is hoping possible." (Paul Pruyser, "Phenomenology and Dynamics of Hoping," *Journal for the Scientific Study of Religion,* Vol. III, No. 1, Fall, 1963, p. 92.)

Psychopathology applies the "reality test" to the hoping that religion generates or fails to generate in the mental patient. Erikson, again, says that both an individual and a religious system of belief may be so frantic in the search for a "hope-giving relationship" that they "end up lost in delusions and addictions." When a religion or an individual cuts itself loose from "living ethics," either may regress to "illusory and addictive promises or empty fantasy." (Erik H. Erikson, *Insight and Responsibility,* p. 155; W. W. Norton & Company, Inc., 1964.) Erikson categorizes the various kinds of psychopathology on the basis of the factor of hope in the following ways. In *delusions,* the patient turns to a fictitious hope unrelated to reality. In *addictions,* the patient turns to an agent that supplies "intense but shortlived hope." In *depression,* the patient abandons hope altogether. (*Ibid.,* p. 181.)

Probing into the developmental sources of hope, Erikson says that "the mutuality of adult and baby is the original source of hope, the basic ingredient of all effective as well as ethical human action." (*Ibid.,* p. 231.) He gives reciprocity and mutuality a religious association as the "Golden Rule in the light of new insight." (*Ibid.,* pp. 219–243.) In the treatment of the mentally ill—and, for that matter, in the teaching of all kinds and conditions of people—the objective is to strike that sympathetic note which produces a resonant response in the patient or the student. If a measure of mutuality can be established and a reciprocity begun, hope is engendered in both the patient and the physician, the student and the teacher.

The problem of unforgiveness and unforgivingness in this book pinpoints the relationship of mutuality of forgiveness and forgivingness to the development of a hopeful and trusting world view that can be called both religious and well. Chapter 6 highlights this dimension of the element of hope in any creative religious life as compared with the element of hopelessness in the sick religion.

LOVE AND LOVELESSNESS IN MENTAL ILLNESS

Another religious factor in mental illness is the deprivation of love, and the religious factor in mental health

is the nutriment of love. The mutuality that engenders
hope is the greater factor of love. The helpless child
responds to the person who accepts responsibility for
him. This acceptance of responsibility is the concretiza-
tion of love. The child learns to trust those who demonstrate that they are dependable. Erikson defines love as
the *"mutuality of devotion forever subduing the antag-
onisms inherent in divided function."* (*Ibid.,* p. 129, italics
his.)

The word "love" is overworked and misunderstood in
the English language. The Greek language is clearer in
its use of different words for love, which help clarify
and summarize much that has been taught by psychotherapists about the implicitly and explicitly religious
factor of love and lovelessness in mental illness and
health. The Greek word *storgē* refers to family love and
love of kindred. Freud pointed out that mental illness
is related to the fixation of adult love at the level of the
parent-child relationship. Religion may aid and abet this
when it becomes a hearthstone religion with no larger
or more comprehensive outlet for growth and maturity.
Under stress an individual may regress to this level of
maturity and thus become sick.

In the second place, the Greek language uses the word
eros to refer to sexual love. The whole psychoanalytic
movement has described the relationship of the sexual
development of a person to his emotional health or
disease. Early psychologists of religion such as Starbuck
and James associated religious conversion with the onset
of puberty and the storm and stress of the sense of guilt
about one's awakened sexual powers. More recently,
Gordon Allport asserted that "to feel oneself meaning-

fully linked to the whole of Being is not possible before puberty." (Gordon Allport, *Becoming,* p. 94; Yale University Press, 1955.) Similarly, even the name of mental disorders, "dementia praecox" epitomizes early psychiatric theory that associated mental illness with the failure of growth in the years just following puberty. Leaving father and mother and cleaving to one's wife is a major personality adjustment as well as a religious command of both the Old and New Testaments.

The Greek word *philia,* in the third place, focuses upon the fraternal love of friend to friend. The developmental task of building an adequate peer group of trustworthy friends with whom one can be intimate without too much threat or suspicion is a third crisis that may turn toward illness or health. Erikson associates this with the first stage of adulthood, when the individual may move toward genuine friendship and intimacy with other people on a durable and trustworthy basis or he may move away from them into self-absorption. Expansiveness of generosity as well as of genitality is one meaning of love, he says. Such capacity is the prerequisite of productivity in creative work. (Erikson, *Identity and the Life Cycle,* p. 96.) In early adulthood, then, the role of religion in illness and health may be measured by the power of a given community to create this fellowship among the adherents of the religious group. However, religion itself may militate against this, and, when it does, it contributes to ill health rather than health-giving relationships.

Finally, the Greek language refers to another kind of love, *agape,* which refers to an unconditional love based on esteem. It follows the direction of the lover's free choice of the loved one for her own sake alone. It excludes the instrumental gain the relationship may afford as a direct or indirect result. *Agape* is not only free in its choice but uncalculating in its hope of gain. Martin Buber distinguished this kind of love as an I-Thou relationship, from an I-It relationship, in which the partners use one another for their own ends. The mentally healthy person is the one who has achieved and received a measure of ability to love in this way. As Harry Stack Sullivan defined maturity, it means to be able to love another person as much as or almost as much as oneself. The direction of mental health is to foster this kind of love. The religious factor in mental disease is the absence of this kind of love.

In addition to detailed discussion that makes clear the factors of the life of faith summarized thus far in this chapter, this book takes a fresh contribution from the area of preventive psychiatry. This is the stress placed upon the importance of the factors of faith, hope, and love at the great transitions of life. Apart from the functional effectiveness of religion at the great crossing points of life, men who espouse religion find it to be a salt that has lost its savor, a broken reed unsafe to rely upon with one's whole life. The word and the sacrament of religion are weighed in the balances and found adequate or wanting in these times of crisis. Again, the whole concept of spiritual territory set forth in this book is a new application of the concepts of behavioral science to the religious life of both sick and well persons. Furthermore, this book hopes to make a fresh contribution at the point of the pathology of religious leadership. The decisions about the wholeness or unwholesomeness of religion can rarely rise above the decisions of its most persuasive and potent leaders. They permit people to be whole insofar as they themselves have participated in wholeness. They protect people from the pathology of religion insofar as they have received this protection themselves.